Education Without Walls

About the Author

Edith Helen Stone-Jackson was born in Detroit, Michigan. She graduated from the Detroit Public School System and was awarded piano certificates from the Royal Conservatory of Music of Toronto, Canada. Leaving home, she chose to attend Eastern Michigan University. Studies in human health at the Aquarian Center in California led her to attain an AS, concentrating on Medical Laboratory Technology from Wayne County Community College in Detroit. She attended many universities and colleges before she graduated from Michigan State University, with a BA from the College of Urban Development. A writing fellowship from University of Nevada, Las Vegas inspired her to attain secondary teaching credentials in both science and social sciences.

Edith was married and raised two children while teaching in Las Vegas, Nevada. She resettled with her family when her husband was stationed in Turkey by the United States Air Forces, where she was invited to teach at the elementary school on Incirlik. She enjoyed the Sulaymaniyah Mountains, Whirling Dervishes, Mediterranean beaches, restaurants and the hospitality of the Turkish people. They were also welcomed in Cyprus and Germany. She later traveled to the Caribbean, Colombia, France, England, Canada, Switzerland, Cameroon and Equatorial Guinea.

Her teaching career allowed Edith to be independent, and talk about chemistry, biology, earth science, physical science, and the research methods and laboratory experiments that she loved. Her Native Americans In Literacy project under Adult Basic Education was designed to add written language to oral stories. The State of Nevada agreed, taking over the literacy project in 1992. Colleagues in her graduate computer science class at Indiana University, Bloomington, in 1998, wholeheartedly supported her project to visit the Koji Indians in the Andes Mountains while teaching in Colombia. Becoming a federal contractor in 2008 allowed her to use her Education Support Services designation to design her solar energy project during President Obama's administration. She was known to fund her own enrichment projects for neighborhood kids. Assigned to underperforming schools, she held students to strict state performance standards as she proudly witnessed the excellence of their growth. Their exceptional progress was her greatest source of joy while teaching. Edith is now retired with the California State Teachers Retirement System, but still takes small contracts, substitute teaches, and writes.

Edith Stone-Jackson

Education Without Walls

Olympia Publishers
London

www.olympiapublishers.com
OLYMPIA PAPERBACK EDITION

A CIP catalogue record for this title is
available from the British Library.

ISBN: 978-1-78830-491-7

This is a work of non-fiction.
Names, characters, places and incidents originate from the writer's
imagination. Any resemblance to actual persons, living or dead, is
purely coincidental.

First Published in 2020

Olympia Publishers
Tallis House
2 Tallis Street
London
EC4Y 0AB
Printed in Great Britain

Dedication

To Ramsey, my son that did not know my story,
our ancestors,
Jacob Stone, his great-great grandfather, his great-grandparents,
and his grandparents.
To all my grandchildren, students, and the Cree Nation.

Acknowledgements

Love is the most great law that ruleth this mighty and heavenly cycle, the unique power that bindeth together the diverse elements of this material world, the supreme magnetic force that directeth the movements of the spheres in the celestial realms. Love revealeth with unfailing and limitless power the mysteries latent in the universe.

Cleanse your eyes so that ye behold no man as different from yourselves.

The teacher should not see in himself any superiority; he should speak with the utmost kindliness, lowliness and humility, for such speech exerteth influence and educateth the souls.

'ABDU'L~BAHA

Dr Bryan Hickman, had it not been for you squeezing this writing out of me, there would be no book. Thank you for forcing me to meet my potential; pushing me to strive until I was out of breath!

Ramsey David Jackson, thank you for giving me the first glimmer that I am not invisible, and providing a beautiful property at which I could write.

David and Phyllis Stone, thank you for battling through segregation for me, with the legacy of my ancestors as a shield and my opportunities as your vision.

Charlaine Cynthia Clay, thank you for being my touchstone.

Dianne DeRouen Robinson, thank you for your 18 years of advocacy, protection, sincerity, 100% accurate clairvoyance, and visualizing this book.

Adrienne Grimes Warren, thank you for 55 years of friendship, and catching me when I had nowhere to fall.

Frankie Franklin, thank you for 57 years of companionship, advice, and caring sisterhood.

Mary Louise Barnes, thank you for getting me to graduation at Michigan State University and being one of the Saints. Thank you for the time you spent hearing what I was saying while writing this book.

David S. Stone, thank you for showing me that I am family.

Curtis Dickerson, thank you for understanding what to do with Mary's loving instructions for the family.

Vicki Scott, thank you for years of technical support and keeping the family laughing.

Dr Albert Ligon (deceased), thank you for 10 degrees Neophyte on my spiritual path, sharing the universal expanse of your knowledge and your personal interest in my development. I found my unction! You are so missed.

Dr Asa Hilliard (deceased), thank you for uninhibited courage and leadership among educators that supported our best strategies to teach African American students. Thank you for your research, for demonstrating how to publish, and your public concern with the well-being of Black teachers and their students. Your absence is felt.

Dr June and Dr Richard Thomas, thank you for demonstrating what marriage can be. Thank you both for welcoming me as professors to the College of Urban Development at Michigan State University, and teaching me the dynamic skills which inform my ability to unpack social institutions. Those form the scaffold onto which this book is hung!

Hazel James, thank you for your kindness, your mentorship and traveling the spiritual path next to me.

Robert Floyd, thank you for your heart. There is no rival in this world to your sensitivity, selflessness and neighborhood fellowship.

John Odell, thank you for the intimacy and affording me the freedom to be Unconstrained as the Wind. Thank you for your research contributed to this book. You are always in my heart.

Foreword

With crystalline hindsight, Edith Stone returns to her youth to make sense of her twilight. Her struggles as a student and instructor, Negro, Black, African American and woman cycle through the misguided trails of the American educational system. Her life is filled with people she has touched, as a result of those who have touched her. There is a journey to be taken with Edith and with painstaking certainty, she ensures we ride her roller coaster intently. If ever I was confused about why, rather than what I was taught and how, rather than why I was taught, I was completely unencumbered at the end of her tale. The innocence of the child rings clearly through these pages, and reminds me of the subtle fears and feelings I repressed. The adolescent confusion is documented well and her resolute decisions to fight as an adult pulse through the readers' veins, as if a return to civil rights is most necessary and inevitable.

It is those of us who were there and experienced the promise of a new day who are entrusted with passing that history along. It is that we might learn whence we came and look forward to where we are headed. It is to understand why the earlier generations are where they are, rather than condemning them for not being further, as so many of us do. It is to understand that if not for them, our worlds would be a mite smaller, and our heads would not reach the heavens so easily.

In keeping with her civic responsibility, Edith has recounted, reconstructed and conveyed where the educational system in the United States began for the minority student. She has illustrated racism, sexism and classism with gritty anecdotes and forbidden facts. She has depicted the emergence from a systematic degradation of disenfranchised students, only to emerge into a practice of systematic corruption. She has depicted that through it all, it is the individual's decision to conduct themselves with dignity, and command the utmost respect through the actions that we all know to be good and integral. These individuals are who we remember most in our lives, and who shape us for the better.

This is a truly enlightening piece, necessary to the framework of scholastic progress, necessary to the commitment to the equalization of education, and necessary to the memory of our nation. Hers is a cog in the wheel of scholastic enterprise. Some came before her and some will come after, but her 60 year span must be remembered and counted if ever we are to be better than what we have accomplished so far.

Ramsey David Jackson

My Days at the Lake

I counted the pebbles at the lake once
Said a prayer for every one
And recalled a story once they were gone
I traded for the whispers
Listening to their clicks on the shells
As they went on about your childhood exploits
Remember, they chatter
That special girl with the pigtails and knobby knees
Running through the forests
In search of tomorrow's memories
I counted the rocks at the lake once
Dreamed of a new world
Where I made my mother proud
Where her sun shone brightly beyond the curtains of the past
And the reality of our future became evident
I listened to the whistle in the trees
Recounting the joyous return of which I was none the wiser
I counted the stones at the lake once
Got to about three
And realized we were all that mattered
Sheltered by each other

Protected from the jealous few that never understood
The ones who never gave a damn what our last name was
Whether we were part of the family or not
Those stones shattered our dreams
And splintered our faith
But these stones are made for building
A home of such grandeur
A stone's throw from a lifetime away
Complete with a white picket fence
And a cobblestone walkway
Muting a stone's insults
Never to count again

The Dream I Had

I must have dreamed about you, years ago
Before the morning dew settled
After the night disappeared
During my training day

I planned my life
Searched for the best
And found it
Moved in
Moved out
And moved on

Prodded by an example
Gauged by my success
You are the surface on which my life reflects

I've grandstanded
Written words worth their weight
And discovered solitude for the simpler things

I learned please and thank you
The nonessential for yellow floppy hair
A child's smile

And birthday wishes from you
Those things I've never forgotten
And always remember
Those things my child covets
Which masticate the world's evils
And make them easier to swallow
Mine is to know I chose well
As my life is only a measure of yours.

The Shelter

Lean-to's with shingle roofs
Back yards and dining rooms
The quarters my soul must mend
You kept us from sun scorched backs
And wind burned lashes
Protected the fragile children the world cast aside
Hiding the growth the world would come to fear
I lead my own charge from its depths
Escaping the inescapable only to return, thankful beyond words
My safety reflects nothing more than the shelter I'm afforded
And repaid only with my own brand of kindness
The world watched as your back sprawled across us
Usurping licks and lashes meant for my sister and me
The uninspired, the uninformed, the unimportant
Generations have thankfully wandered under the canopy
Safe from the rain and hail
And emerged a new breed
Strong in mind, stern in will
Ours is the shame too common
The world's skeleton
The wonder given reasons by the fearless fairy
Guiding the hands of time

Blessing the dregs with that which they deserve
Sheltering the few
Huddling the masses
And promising the world a triumphant return

Prelude

In this course, I will share many of the ideas that I researched during that time. It would take many lifetimes to discover the details of our record of human existence from 3.6 million years ago until now. In order to deal more effectively with each other in current times though, we need to become more familiar with our common evolution, socially and psychologically. In our study, we can make use of some existing bodies of information.

When individuals look at their places in society, many more considerations exist than meet the eye. Taking the Implicit Associative Tests will expose blind spots that we all develop, resulting from living in families that exist in various societies. Our preferences creep into our personalities randomly, without our conscious consent. All the warmth and love of a family does not prevent bias from prevailing in human interactions. Sometimes our comfortable preferences preclude us from experiencing as peaceful an existence as we would like. By delving into our unconscious thinking, we will be aided in overcoming some social obstacles. Social stumbling seems harmless enough, but it can become problematic when others become unbearably uncomfortable by it.

Right here is a good place to stop reading and go to <implicit.harvard.edu>. Taking these tests should motivate us all to change some of our behaviors that are offensive to others. Small changes in a great number of individuals can bring us closer to peace. Please take the race bias test now and once again **after** finishing this book (It will coincide with tracing the genetic composition during human migration on earth).

The Backdrop

It was not until 2016 that I shared with my daughter that the only representation I ever had in school of a Black person was about this little brown boy in a white loin cloth, chased by a tiger, who loved pancakes. Oh yeah, I squealed out, the story of *Little Black Sambo*. Well, Krystal squealed too, but in disbelief. She had never known anyone who had ever even seen that book. She was instantly offended, and began asking people in the store she was in if anyone had ever heard of that story. Wasn't it banned? She turned to the 28-year-old store clerk waiting on her, Leonard, and asked, "Have you ever heard of the book, *Little Black Sambo*?" Leonard and some folks in line recalled the book and that it had been banned for being racist. They were all loud about it, feeling sorry that I been put through this ordeal as a child. I never thought of it like that.

Well, I missed that memo. Right then, telling my daughter about what happened registered in my mind why the Civil Rights Movement came to Detroit! I was the only Black kid in that class, and as an educated adult, I now realize that it is not legal to single out persons due to race to make them look and feel insufficient. I further explained to my daughter, Krystal, that it was a great story in my mind, because I loved buttery pancakes as much as

Sambo did! She and all in the store cracked up laughing at the innocence I brought to being told a story by my teacher. Surely the teacher wanted to impress and entertain my class. But when, at the end of the story, she turned to me and asked where little black Sambo came from, I was quite embarrassed. I had nothing new or interesting to gain the interest of the white kids, who were all looking at me, waiting to hear something magnificent.

Wanting to know what I could have contributed, I told my mother the story when I got home. A white woman too, my mother marched furiously up to the school right then, and got right up close on the teacher so she could explain what I should have said! It all got pretty sputtery between the teacher and the principal, when they realized my mother had enough sense to be offended. My mother let 'em have it that day.

I never made the connection between this experience and what happened before we even moved into our newly built house. I was confused by the white kids in the area, when they confessed to my father that they had been responsible for breaking out the windows and taking a poop on the new floor. After being confronted, they never came back and never made friends with us.

The Bonners lived next door when we moved in on Woodingham Drive. A few years older than me, Susan would jump rope in front of her old shabby house. I wanted to learn how, so I would go outside to join in every time I saw she was outside. She stopped letting me have a turn, and then she started ignoring me. In a few more days, she was made to stay in their yard. In a few more days, well within 10 to 15 minutes of us being out at the same time, her mother would belt out, "Susan, time to come in now". My mother took the mystery out of it when she told me Susan's mother did not want her to play with me because they were white. In a few months, the Bonners had moved into an even more rural area. The old white lady across the street bragged to my father where they went. Daddy must have looked it up to find their address. Our family rode out there one day, and much to my father's sense of humor, he exclaimed, "They bought a house exactly like ours!"

My 5th grade science teacher told my mother that my problem was that I was just too aggressive. He had sent me to the principal's office several times for talking too much. At 10 years old, I couldn't understand the meaning of "aggressive" in reference to myself. At 65 years old, it took a lot for me to dredge up these instances and connect the title *discrimination* to them.

By comparison, I remember Mrs Paschal had taught science in my school since 1st grade. She was exciting, and had anyone interested in all her animals, pets and displays join the Science Club. My classmate Linda took me with her, so I could believe it was true. Mrs. Paschal would chatter with us about the nature of science with every question we'd ask her. She let us feed the animals, water the plants, ask about class assignments. She even took us on the only class trip. We took a bus to an exhibit at Cobo Hall. She was Irish and even had us over to her home to meet her family and have a succotash dinner!

As an adult science teacher, I was asked how I had gotten into science education. I smiled when I thought back. I had never really realized before that Mrs. Paschal was the only teacher who rewarded us for our enthusiasm for learning in her class. No one got sent to the principal for talking.

My father was determined for us to learn science as well. On the weekends he would sit us at the kitchen table to teach us scientific concepts: visible and invisible, the revolution of the earth and its orbit around the sun, multiplication tables, cold and heat effects, pressure, gravity, centrifugal force, measurement.

I missed my 5th grade science fair project. Daddy found out when I got a failing grade in science. He introduced me to metallurgy. He was a journeyman metallurgist at General Motors in Detroit. I demonstrated that I knew my metals and their characteristics in the report I wrote, and in the samples Daddy provided to me to glue onto my project whiteboard.

And then there was my trusted social studies teacher. Mr Curtis threw me into a tizzy because I used to love this young, energetic, tall, blonde, blue-eyed man. When he called on my raised hand, I asked him, seriously, why Africa was never mentioned. He began telling me that Africans didn't have any history and didn't contribute anything to the world. In front of the whole class, he presented that I, as well as where I had come from, had no past. I felt invisible, defeated and became ambivalent toward Mr Curtis.

On the bright side, my father began to change the way we acted and thought. He began to take the whole family down to the Art Institute on Sundays after church, to the Study of Negro Life and History. Could anything be more boring? It was a long and tiring day. My father and brother would leave there very inspired, sharing the secrets they had learned about how much history Negroes had contributed to the world, contrary to what Mr Curtis had told us in my social studies class.

My mother whose race is questionable, knew how these race games were played, because it had happened to her. She knew that she would have to prove to the principal my grades were calculated incorrectly in order to get my correct grade.

Racism has it so that anyone of either race can gain favor with the dominant group by harming the Negro. She also knew that they were allowing the new Negro kids to beat on me and steal from me, because all this disruption never took place when the Jews attended school with me. The moral code evaporated right along with the absent whites.

Time and time again, when I would think back to these stinging events during a course I took with University of California San Diego, it would become clear to me that I had been racially harassed as a child. That six-year-old Sarah's mother could be permitted to holler in my face not to play with her daughter anymore, was more shocking to me. Using lies to force my mother to come to the school, by telling her upsetting tales about me caused me to be spanked. One of my problems, explained by Mrs Mitzifeld was supposed to have been that, "teacher is always wrong and Edith is always right". This choreographed lie showed me even the principal was in on this strategy to defame me. I frantically thought, how far up the ladder does this web of deceit go?

My refuge from the pressure at school was that my parents never really monitored my whereabouts in those slow, late 1950s days. So, I'd be all over, about a square mile, on my bike. I'd be going in the stores, noticing what merchandise I planned on getting for 25 cents to a dollar. Of course, I noticed the lunch counter. I'd go sit up to it on my swivel stool among the adults. The waitress would always tell me to move down in case any adults needed a quick space. Finally, she would come down to me and take my hotdog or grilled cheese order.

By the time 1963 slid in, I had a new friend, Renita. The only child of a new couple in the neighborhood was introduced to my parents at the Raglands' party. Her color of black was highly reactive among the brown girls, living in the colonial residential homes. They kept bringing it up as if it could be corrected. Renita would have me meet her for lunch at Kresge's and afterward, we would both hop on the bus that ran past the big store window. The only thing was, Renita would never approach the counter to eat. After the long walk to the store, I'd want to sit down to eat. She would order with me and then quickly go stand up at the small round tables with no seats.

It all worked itself out when, in a few months, my mother told me Martin Luther King Jr was heading up a boycott. This meant not eating in Kresge's for a while and not riding the bus either. I never remembered the bad counter service at Kresge's as hurtful. Again, I dismissed it, as adults having the right to eat first because they worked. Looking back, I would have been such a good candidate for chattle slavery, because I was never suspicious!

College was a question in the back of my mind. My mother always said I was going, but did Civil Rights just a couple of years ago mean I would really go? Could I use Kresge's five and dime store as the example of a muddled future? Suddenly, they, all my white friends, were gone when I entered Hampton Jr. High, without any explanation. My middle school Latin teacher, Mrs Greenberg, had several tactics familiar to me; to discourage and degrade. As children, we don't know that we are the targets of such elaborate plots to demolish our entire lives. I'm glad I didn't know. As a child, I continued to respect and admire my teachers, because I didn't know any better. I remember how red her face turned and how much spittle formed on her lips when she told the class off for letting my grades end up so much better than theirs. Mostly Jewish kids, such as herself, she let them retest and I noticed from then on, I would have a failing grade. In 1965, I was able to figure out her methods. She'd give the highest points for all the questions I got wrong, then mark on a curve which made my grade drop but the other's soar. It slipped out one afternoon that she met the Jewish kids at the after school program at Sharey Zedek Hebrew School, where all their school work was explained and corrected with them. Jewish kids would begin to be pulled out of classes with Negroes and put together in isolation, so that their grades, in every class, soared to the top of the whole school. Segregation is what it was called.

She called me to her desk at the end of the year and made me promise never to take another Latin class. If I promised, she said she'd pass me. Who could I tell on her? Her wardrobe told me she was a powerful Jew. Nobody messed with her!

My new Negro friend, Yvonne, and I didn't challenge how mean she was in class. Curiously, nobody talked against her. We admired her expensive gold set jewelry in which there were sapphires, rubies, pearls, emeralds and every other precious stone. She never wore the same suit twice in the entire year, and these were from the expensive Jewish dress shops like Jacobson's, B. Siegle's, and Winkleman's, up on the Avenue of Fashion.

About 80 years old, by the time I got to 10th grade, she'd hobble down the hall (on the wrong side) in her matching leather shoes on her way to class…honey blonde hair perpetually in place. I was more than surprised and delighted, too, when I spotted her hobbling down the hall at my new high school. I felt proud that I knew such a woman when I spoke to her loudly in the hall at Mumford High. She greeted me respectfully this year and I felt a warmth about her, as we kids all did, so I took Spanish with her. I had been a witness that she knew her stuff. By this time, white flight was over and I had lost every Jewish and white friend I had ever made. I didn't know it then, but I had felt discouraged and detached from the rambunctious Negro kids moving into the deserted houses the whites had left behind. Nobody saw fit to address this devastation with all the kids also that had left or been deserted. I had no drive to learn anything anymore. In a quiet state of rebellion, I think Mrs Greenberg noticed I was only doing just enough work to get by. She was much softer with me, as if we both despised this loss.

A pretty girl named Karmen Harlin was in that class. She was the hopeful, driven student that I had been once as a child, while surrounded by my best friends at Pasteur Elementary School. A quiet girl, she didn't make friends with me. She became a news anchor woman when we grew up, who still never talked with me.

Short in height, tightly twisted French roll up the back of the head, Ms Jaanosi softly spoke accented English everyday during her lectures. Her starched white lab coat made her appear serious about teaching biology. Her presentation made us take her seriously, as well as, biology. Looking back, I can see that white flight left teaching positions empty, business buildings empty, houses and school desks empty.

It felt like college in her class. Mrs Jaanosi challenged us with that thick biology text, and outlined detailed labs we would do. I still think about her explaining the behavior and eye color of fruit flies to us, as if it was her whole life. But the lab day we pithed frogs' brains to prepare them for dissection, we drifted back to our writing tables when done. Penny was standing there, by her chair, among us.

Having what now would be called a nervous breakdown, Penny passionately rambled out a shocking story. As tears streamed down her cheeks, she pleaded her case. Her family required her to get all As, because she was a Jew. She owed it to her grandparents because they had been in concentration camps during the extermination holocaust. We had known each other since first grade, but the distance between us felt explained by the tears streaming down her face.

Speechless, what was I supposed to do for Penny and all the Jews I loved? I never knew this tragic motivator among them. Helpless, I felt guilty for not knowing. Wondering what the teacher would do, she looked like a stone-chiseled statue. At least she had treated us all fairly, I thought.

In 12th grade, Mr Jaaksi demonstrated only two chemistry labs for us that year. The world's worst teacher also demonstrated, by his lack of competency, what a "ghetto" school would be like. He came late, frumpled, with his coffee thermos and newspaper. No notes ever appeared on the board. He never talked about the Periodic Table, although the standard wall chart was hung for us all to see. We remained on chapter one for the whole year. Most of the kids used his class to tell jokes, laugh and do homework for other classes.

By the time I got to his class, I was just real relieved to be almost done. Like Janet's mother would soon point out, it would show on our transcripts as a college prep requirement met for college, whether I knew anything or not. As a teacher myself, I now understand that man had no intention of teaching us anything and must have also known, nobody was going to make him.

In 1968, I met my 12th grade sociology teacher. Mr White was the new Negro teacher. Unlike Mr Jaaksi, class began on time, with everyone feeling secure that there would be a challenging lesson which included lecture, text references and lively discussion. He was tall and interesting, so smart—and he was also a Negro. He explained to us an idea that we had never heard of, so we leaned in to listen to what sociology was all about. He was the only teacher that could corral us and deliver something new and exciting. So straight laced, yet so approachable, it was a great relief to finally ever get a Negro teacher in an academic subject. He understood our circumstances immediately.

The 1969 yearbook, the Capri, was the yearbook in which he is described in the faculty section. "With Mr Blake White as instructor, the sociology class studied the development, structure, function, and institutions of human society through the ages." At 65 years old, I stumbled upon this description of his duties and upon his signature in my Capri at the time of my graduation in 1969. It brought a long overdue smile to my face, because I had become him: a high school teacher with a major in 'the development, structure, function and institutions of human society through the ages'.

We students promised him that we would continue on studying sociology in college. Well, Mr White's last words to me, over his signature in the Capri yearbook had simply been, "success and happiness".

I continued to feel like a misfit in my own school district. Classes were segregated, whites from the Negroes. I was told by my counselor that all the white kids in those classes were honor students, and that I would only be able to get into a junior college when I graduated. She was a light-skinned Negro, defaulting into gate keeper against other Negroes by getting as close to the whites as she pretended to be. Segregation would be protected by her without even explaining what was happening to me. In the highest 1% in my school on the SAT, I would suppose that she would have recognized my college entrance potential. In those years, being eligible for the National Merit Scholarship was based on race and parental income. The National Merit Scholarship for Negro Students was set apart by race. It was explained that my parents' income was too high to allow me to receive any money. Before Affirmative Action, the other Negro kids that got it finished undergraduate college studies before I did. So, was I being compared to the white kids or to the other Negroes?

But what I had learned up to then, I could have never been taught. It had been an experiment in the subtleties of keeping Black students from white-only opportunities. My 5th grade Jewish friend, Hannah passionately told me I would have to make a choice between the Blacks and the whites I had known since I was six. I told her I would not be forced to make such a choice. She didn't return to school for 6th grade.

So controversial were the mistakes that had been taught to me in Detroit's public schools that I couldn't graduate soon enough. Personally, I didn't know very many Negroes who had graduated college to tell me how I should react to the dozen or so recruitment letters I got in the mail, two years after the Civil

Rights Act was passed into law. It still pains my soul that I didn't understand what those letters meant. In 1968, a seventeen-year-old had four more years to become an adult at twenty-one, which means that some adult should have explained my options for leaving home in acceptance of those offers. Although I had high scores on the college entrance exams, I did not perceive the impact these colleges were trying to make on my life. No adult from school or at home expressed congratulations for my test scores, recruitments or scholarships. No one inquired about my life long plans, as though I had been invisible. So inflamed by the school system, I was a confused mess by the time I graduated. My mother had claimed she and my father would be paying for me, so I applied to Eastern Michigan University with my friends, never acknowledging the colleges offering scholarships. I found out from them very late in my life that they didn't understand the cost of education any better than I did!

That 1969 graduation summer, the closest I got to a serious conversation about myself was talking to my girlfriends. We'd walk from house to house chatting.

I thought back with a new pair of eyes, loaned to me by Janet. I did pass biology, taught by the new foreign teacher from Austria. The first thing I remember was what a pristine professional she was—and fair. I was relaxed in her class. You got to keep all the high grades she gave without her trying to figure out how to cheat you.

My friend Janet led me to think back about how I must look on paper, and what I had endured to get this far. I was a National Merit Scholar. In those days they would do a cut-off, so that Negro students would be in a separate group of scholars. So, it was "National Merit for Negro Scholarships". So, what did that mean? No one bothered to explain it. Not even was it explained at graduation, where the white students were formally congratulated, but me and the other handful of other Negro students were not recognized at all.

That summer, in 1969, we girls all talked about our plans for the future. Janet shared that her mother warned her to get into the sciences, because the competition would be less. There would be more chances for Negroes. She said that even though we had struggled along in college prep sciences in high school, we were still better prepared than the average student. Janet said she was thinking about a laboratory career. So when I got to Eastern Michigan University in the summer of 1969, I took Janet's mother's advice and took two science classes. I ran into Janet about 30 years later in the airport. She had gone into a career with the insurance industry, making good money for sure.

Wendy, the new student from the old neighborhood that I helped get settled in at Pasteur, must remember 5th grade to 12th grade with me. She and her mother attended the meeting in the school library with my mother and me. She did not want to be my friend either. When I was assigned to show her to her locker when she was a new 5th grader at Pasteur Elementary School, she ignored me. Straight through middle school, high school and university with me. Maybe she was right to stick with the Jews and well-dressed Negroes. After law school, she won many elections to be a judge in the City of Detroit.

But did she, or any of the other students, see more than I did about race discouragement growing up? By the time 5th grade rolled around, all my real friends were gone. Things had changed more and more for me, as I floated along through school. All these new Negro kids took over all that was meant for me. At least, that's how I felt. Pushed to the background.

I remembered the tactics used against me as I flashed back: Little Black Sambo, making me be last to draw from the Christmas grab bag, last in the bathroom line, using up all the time promised for me to present my Christmas play, lying to my mother about my behavior in class, not calling on me when my hand was raised, showcasing all countries except African ones. Pulling me out of class so that Mrs Lapedis could scream in my face during her daughter's birthday party, seating me by disruptive, violent students, segregating the classes, accusing me of being jealous of the rich girls' clothes. These are the ways children are destroyed.

It was not until 2016 that I realized something profound about the Civil Rights struggle in Motown. My Union Rep, Diane DeRouen took me to "Motown, the Musical" in San Jose. Memories flooded my mind while I watched as an adult. I never knew segregation was bad with all the glamorous acts I and all the Black children of Detroit craved every Christmas: Willie Tyler and Lester, The Miracles, Supremes, Temptations, Martha and the Vandellas, Mary Wells, Tammy Terrell, Marvin Gaye, Little Stevie Wonder, The Marvelettes, the Four Tops, Moms Mabley, Red Foxx. I realized as a grown person that Motown had enveloped us kids, hoisting us above the hair-raising banter of the daily death toll in the Vietnam War, Civil Rights killings, sit-ins, demonstrations, fire hoses, lynchings, riots, German Shepherd dogs clawing people down. We sang and danced with Berry Gordy's legendary artists on the radio. We partied our way through this madness to single 45s, and at the Motown Review during winter break from school. We were insulated from the terror of the marches and sit-ins, police dog attacks, white police billy clubs, job loss, lynchings, car jackings and even our parent's preoccupation with the anguish.

After the tear-jerking show, it felt like we all wanted to thank Berry Gordy, and wondered if he had been aware that he was taking care of the nation's children by providing a beautiful escape. All of us, white and black, 50, 60 and 70 year olds sat in an integrated audience and cried and sang and clapped together. He needs a Nobel Peace Prize for that!

Unity

It was this very rugged but refined strength that was handed down to me, and supported in the teachings of Eric Butterworth, who came on morning radio back at our old house in 1955. Eric was Unity Minister, and my father took me to be taught in his Sunday School when I was big enough. He'd walk me down the stairs to the basement and drop me at the nursery door.

Self began to make sense to me in resonance to positive affirmations, Bible readings and class discussions over the next ten years. These ten years in the basement galvanized me into believing that I was part of a human experience, where God was on my side. I never suspected that my religious conditioning would prove so controversial among whites. They had learned another brand of who I was, and who I should be. The two ideologies about me would bitterly clash later, as desegregation became law.

As I studied through my primary grades in church, my mother noticed my brother and I had not received the complimentary Bible that all the 99% white kids had. She visited the Sunday School Superintendent's office to protest the treatment she saw as discriminatory. He defended himself by submitting to my mother that our attendance needed not to have any absences for 12 straight Sundays before we would qualify. Something she fired back I would always be proud of. She made the case that we should be entitled because she was a nurse on rotating shifts at the biggest hospital in Detroit. She worked the trauma units, during which she was not always able to get us ready, but she would try by trading off with my father. They reached that compromise, after which I did notice a change in this white man's compassionate smiles toward my brother and me…

It did feel funny when Daddy had to get us dressed up for Easter on his own. He kept looking back over his shoulder at us in the car, as if he was second guessing his own ability to get it right about how we looked. I remember a cream-coloured dress with small white flowers in the fabric. To top it off, it came with a red velvet belt. With that outfit, there was no mistake possible!

The rides to Unity Temple wound through Sherwood Forest and Palmer Park. On this route, church began to already happen. I'd wonder what the Jewish kids of department store owners, Hollywood movie writers, lawyers and doctors were doing in their mansions. Friday worshippers, those sleepy kids would be dropped off by their chauffeurs to Pasteur Elementary School on Monday morning. They'd never know I had ridden by, or that I had viewed their maids on their way home, in starched white uniforms, standing in line at the bus stops. (In fact, when my mother stopped by my school one day straight from the hospital, the kids had asked me if she was a maid). My mother began to come home and change out of her nursing uniform after that.

At church, I had been held out of the Youth of Unity section in my 9th grade year by Mrs Powell. Because 9th grade in our neighborhood was serviced by Hampton Junior High School instead of Mumford High, she insisted on telling me no. I was not eligible to be promoted out of the basement. The high schoolers met in the small chapel upstairs.

By now, only a few white kids were left at our church. These church families had also left in accordance with "white flight". In only one or two years, whites left their churches, stores, homes, schools, businesses, synagogues and friends, as they deserted Detroit.

I'd hear in class at school, as the teacher asked where they were going while taking roll. When they announced with great relief where they were going in the new semesters, I'd be grown before I could place Oak Park, Southfield, Bloomfield Hills, Orchard Lake, Allen Park, Grose Pointe or Harper Woods. I'd look around bewildered that most would be gone from church and school, and not friends with me anymore. They began to ignore me and chatter together about their new lives. An influx of strange kids, with conspicuous ways, would rush into school to take their place.

My first encounter with this new group was in the auditorium with Ms Mitzifeld, the principal. She'd always appear in the doorway to dismiss the quietest groups to the lunchroom across the hall. In the 5th grade, when it should have been cinch for my class to be first, I just sat there, watching her as she looked over the crowd in disgust. These Black kids were running all over, bumping into each other, screaming at the top of their voices, laughing, talking and horse-playing loudly. Mrs Addison and Mrs Allen kept signaling the principal with worried and horrified glances, until old Mitzi had to yell out that no one with their behavior would be getting any lunch unless they could calm down and behave. She had to yell out every demand because they were so hard to control. I felt sorry for the old girl for the first time.

The behavior carried on over into the classroom. These new kids from Carver Elementary could barely read. It seems as though their families were targeted in the Ferndale housing projects, to be the first time home owners of the old houses from which the whites had run off. The whole neighborhood had become packed with these backward learners. Striving for excellence was over. They wanted to fight, gossip, disrupt and challenge the teachers. Mrs Berman, the female physical education teacher, became even more withdrawn and aloof. I had no idea how withdrawn and aloof I also became, while trying to make sense out of what-in-the-world was happening to me around me.

By the time I went to high school in the 10th grade, more Negro kids had surged from the inner city. Frankie Franklin's mother took her out of Mumford. I asked to be transferred out as well, but not enough effort was put in by my family. The school gave me and my mother the run around about transferring me to another school. Even though they lived on the corner of my street, Mrs Franklin transferred Frankie to the beautiful new high school in the small town over from us, about a mile away. Mrs London sent my friends, Marilyn and Brenda, to Girls Catholic Central High School. My favorite cousin in Detroit, Cindy, was shipped off to her grandmother for high school.

Even though there was that influx of Black worshippers at Unity Temple, it remained a solid learning environment. We thank Moses and Elba Powell for maintaining that order. They planned egg dyeing for Easter, the choir for Christmas, music and activities for service, road trips to Canada, annual summer conference train rides to Lee Summit, Missouri, service projects for the church and sick and shut in. They continued to encourage and expect excellence in attendance, appropriate reverence, respectfulness and dutiful attitudes. Nobody dared get out of line with them, especially if you thought you were going on the weekend trips with the group. The YOU. (Youth of Unity—church group for youth, age fourteen to twenty-one) was extra special, because many of the kids that attended also went to high school with me.

Mrs Powell always appeared to be skeptical of me, as she studied the character of each kid under her advisement. She was conscious of integrating with hostile whites, so she made sure of us keeping our hair straightened, legs greased, speech white and quiet. She was not going to stand for any of us Negroes making a spectacle. The Unity doctrine had grown into the very core of me from the nursery, so my religious assumptions proved to flabbergast her. That Jesus Christ was a rabble-rouser, and that there were no such things as mistakes because of predestination, were two such ideas that unnerved her. Elected as the President of YOU at seventeen, I mounted the podium each Sunday ready to lead the group of teens in worship. Her uneasiness caused me to be able to support my assertions with studying the Bible on my own. Jesus brought Civil Rights leaders, such as Stokely Carmichael and Malcom X to life for me as heroic.

With "colored", non-offensive Mrs Powell a nurturing spirit, I got the opportunity to show my strength (in spite of a nasty case of scarring acne all over my face and back). She knew we all needed to go to college, so she cultivated us. Slightly bucked, my front teeth were broken into two points, so that the boys at school had no problem laughing at my shabby clothing and making fun of my dog teeth. Nobody made fun of me at church. When we began to include Youth of Unity groups from Toronto, Canada, I fit in well. This is how I met Gary Gilmour, and a girl named Mel.

Under the Powells, every teenager we met from Canada was white, probably with English ancestry. They'd stay at our houses in the US and we'd stay at their houses in Canada. Our favorite conversation topics were school, records, dances, fashion, boyfriends and plans for the future, just like the other Negro church kids. Mel left church with me to sleep over my house one fall weekend in 1965.

I thought my family was a little quiet and standoffish. It actually gave me more time to enjoy the company of Mel privately. That Sunday morning when we were leaving for church, it was freezing cold. Mel had put on a short sleeved, light weight dress. I offered her a brand new red coat that I had just gotten for Easter the previous spring. Turning blue with cold, she refused to put the coat on. She rode all the way to church without a coat.

Momma said she didn't want to put on a coat after a Negro. With its emphasis on positive thinking and race equity, I do not recall one single individual referring to race at church for my whole life, except my mother. The idea of prejudice in connection to any of my church friends sounded out of place to me. That remark only served to portray my mother as misguided. I never knew what caused Mel to reject wearing my coat, but felt it was a stupid move because what did it prove? Only that she was the only one freezing cold!

When Mel brought me to her quaint-looking little London neighborhood in Canada, she yelled out to her mother while opening the door to their warm home. In a plain cotton house dress, her mom rushed to meet me, smiling and inquiring about Mel's day, getting me to the house. Quite a humble being, the mother offered hot tea back in the kitchen, amused by two teenagers so excited about growing up.

Mel had a crush on a handsome boy in Detroit named Lance. The year after the Civil Rights law was signed, our friendships with these white Canadians had required no adjustment. Between us, the 1960s conjured no mistrust or enmity. Gary and I wrote to each other every week as we always had, and Mel's mother never prevented her from that crush she had on the Negro Lance from Detroit.

One of the most vicious life lessons I ever learned would be my hardest to accept. It felt as though, wherever I went, everyone was standing in water, holding onto an electric cord. My behavior was so uncustomary as a brown-skinned person that it became the plugged-into-socket moment, which caused everyone to be electrocuted. How was it, all my life, that my grades were miscalculated, that trucks would run me off the road, that unusual requirements for employment surfaced for me, that my light bill would double over white neighbors, that job tenure and home loans would be withheld, as was enforcement of orders for child support? To look at just these few examples, who would believe that I was an American citizen!

Daddy Said

When we moved from 18655 Charest to the new house, it was during the cold winter month of January 1957. That spring I remember the Black Muslims dropping by, to sit at our dining room table and indulge my father in lengthy, dry, boring conversations that I'd be glad would be over with. Daddy remembered that the Black Muslims made a good point about the Negro converting. They would treat you better than the Christians did. Other nights, static laden radio broadcasts came into the house, communicating the progress of Jomo Kenyatta and Kwame Nkrumah, who were organizing against the British for freedom and independence. What did this undercurrent of adult talk have to do with life, I thought.

My father sat all dressed up one Sunday afternoon and told us to stay inside. He and Momma were going to the Masonic Temple to hear Dr Martin Luther King speak. Whenever he would speak on television, we were all shushed to listen.

Daddy's personal opinions on segregation and oppression never came across my mind, until I went to the musical play with Diane DeRouen. While I was sitting there in the audience, something that I couldn't put my finger on jabbed at me. In the background on stage, scenery connected what events were coinciding with the music with which we were so mesmerized. I would need to inquire from my father how he was reacting to the discrimination and oppression at that same time.

At 65 years old, in 2016, I called Daddy and asked him just that. Why had I not thought of asking this straight forward question before? I thought I knew just because… what he told me was shocking.

Before Motown, he explained, the Black churches kept Black people sane. The congregation would sing songs about freedom, "Go down Moses, let my people go…" I could visualize all those old 33 rpm albums in the basement of spiritual songs, by Negro artists like Mahalia Jackson. He said the church was also hesitant to integrate, because what would a white girl do if she wanted to marry a Negro who could not get a job to support her in the style of her parents? Poor whites held on to the tail of rich whites so they could claim superiority over Negroes. That way they would be able to continue on claiming the jobs. Desegregation would cause too many problems for everyone, because of all the readjustments that may not even work. Just being up out of the south was a blessing for northern Negroes, although they did feel real sorry for those left back.

I was shocked by Daddy's enthusiasm. He shared things he had never told me before. I knew he had graduated from Cass Technical High School, the best in Detroit. But in 2016, he told me more of what happened in 1945. Two hundred white car factory workers had surrounded him in the Detroit Diesel cafeteria while chanting, "Get the nigger out!" He had been promoted to the journeyman track, but now found himself trapped on top of a lunch table, fending for his life. It was so loud the Union Rep ran in and told them, "You don't have to work with David Stone, but you'll all be in the army tomorrow morning! No more exemptions for you!"

When Daddy's older brother, Raymond, heard the story, he pulled out his Smith and Wesson pistol. "Strap this to your leg, David, if you go back in there." I got a cold chill just to hear these details. Daddy turned it over in his mind and decided, "I'd rather die a Christian if they kill me. I won't fight." When he got back to work, his Negro buddy, James Overton, told him he was right. "Beat them at their own game. Put in double the money they do whenever the collection pot for anybody is taken up. Then, they have to think twice!" That guy made sense and agreed with the Bible verse, "treat your enemies with love." Daddy and his buddy won. When the factory found out David Stone was getting married, they bought him a beautiful quilt, after realizing they had been misled into hating the Blacks. He and Momma saved that quilt without using it for many years because it meant so much, coming from these once hateful white men.

Daddy said, by 1964, when Civil Rights was put into the law book, there was no real change in anybody's situation. The poor whites kept holding onto the tail of the big horse of rich whites. They thought if they held on tight enough, they could claim a status in society based on just merely being white, too.

While we talked, I reminded Daddy of the time we went to the Sunday afternoon matinee show downtown. Stopped by the usher, he told us we were not allowed to sit down. We had to go upstairs. As Daddy carried me he asked the usher if he really expected him to carry me all the way upstairs to the balcony. We struggled uncomfortably that Sunday, so we never went back downtown for anything else, ever again.

Daddy recalled Benny Billingslea from 1930. He was one of the first Black starters for the Detroit bus company, called "green hornets". They were responsible to follow the buses to make sure they were on time. It was an important job, because the starters had to have a 17 jewel pocket watch. No Black man ever had that requirement, but Benny did!

I wondered how Daddy felt about all the Black southerners left back there. Was there a kinship, goals for their recovery, feelings of doom or anger about them? In a quieter tone, Nesbit Patten was brought up. In 1935, he had been such an exceptionally smart teenager that he got into college at an early age. He got some fellows into the NAACP and would meet Daddy at the library. He talked about boycotting neighborhood stores and other businesses, but none of the neighbors would cooperate. They were afraid of hurting their own living conditions. They felt removed from the South, and better off. They were just happy not being in the South anymore, because conditions in the North were so much better.

These discoveries I was making about my father's past were quite reminiscent of my Gran Gran. At nine years old, she told me she had a secret to tell me that I should never share. Her great-grandfather, Teakle, had been a conductor on the Underground Railroad. I had to promise not to tell anyone, because we might need that passage out of the United States again. In 2015, I looked up this Teakle on the internet. The story was actually there. He and his white brothers had built the biggest, finest house in Maryland. The article stated it was a rumour that he had journeyed slaves through the property, and onto the river into freedom. I knew these freed slaves and their white conductors as family. I laughed out loud!

It felt like Daddy had withheld his information on purpose, because we might need his type of silence again too, regarding Joe Jones. Joe Jones reminded me of the actor, Eammon Walker, from "Chicago Fire" on TV. A dashing, confident advocate, he had Daddy and other working Negro men collect money. Joe Jones would send it back down South to Martin Luther King to fund the Civil Rights Movement down there. There was the "glass ceiling" on jobs, so Negroes were not serious about education. They had to help Dr King, because they knew the excuses they would hear when they applied for jobs in the Detroit area. "Sorry, the job was just filled, but you can stay on the list." This is what would be said to Negro applicants. But behind them, in that same line, the whites were being shuttled into jobs with no apology. No one would ever get back in touch with Negroes on the waiting list. In my mind's eye, I could see the big man when Daddy described that the "Peck-a-wood tried to cut him in line. Joe Jones balled up his fist and knocked him down." Nothing went well for Joe Jones after that at Diesel. He became so controversial that he left Diesel.

Maybe he could do better, like Edsel Hart. Edsel was one of the first Negroes to get a job with the Detroit bus company in 1939. He drove the Dexter bus line. In that white neighborhood, he was so resented that one day a white woman spat on him. Wherever Negroes lived, the jobless fear existed.

Looking back, I realize Daddy was lock stepping with Dr Martin Luther King Jr, in what the road to greater freedom would look like. It meant Daddy would boldly activate his own viability amidst the other Negroes in his circle, by becoming a role model of dignity, unity and strength. He was just that, brave Christian, brave parent and authentic friend to all the people who knew us in the fifties and sixties. There was not a time that he didn't rush out the door to lend a hand to a neighbor moving in, or share a listening ear with the men struggling to provide for their families.

Daddy stocked our own freezer with ice cream and hotdogs, and the cupboards with all kinds of desserts, pretzels, nuts and chips. We certainly were not going to miss eating at Kresge's lunch counter. He put a drop-in record player in the counter in the basement, an enclosed television and movie screen in the walls. He wallpapered the walls with red wall paper that featured musical notes, keyboards and saxophones in black and white.

Daddy took us to see the movie about Minnesota Fats when he brought the fine new pool table into the basement, with Mr. Binion's help (Had the grownups been talking about boycotts together at one of those parties?). The new pool table, with a dropped down fluorescent light fixture he installed above it was exactly like the movie. He made a cue stick rack. He set up our table tennis, and with finality, the basement was crowned with the juke box. Colored lights that flickered inside it excited us all. We loved dropping in a penny to buy a song selection to dance to. Brook Benton, Perry Como, Elvis, Nat King Cole, Brenda Lee, the Four Seasons, singing from the juke box, and you'd think you were in the fantasy land of any rich white family. After 1957, no white kids ever came over to visit anymore…

We Negro kids would play the Motown hits in ours and other family friends' basements. Neighbors like the Eatons, the Feltons, the Franklins, the Grimes, the Londons, the Hargroves, were happy to let their kids enjoy the music and space to dance and sing. Families and friends of friends from Bishop Hancock's Sanctified Holiness Church; the Raglands, the Clements, the

Howards, the Conwells, the Kanoytons, the Pattersons valued this sheltered and upstanding environment, where fun could be had, free of ill repute. All the family joined in, on both sides; from the Watsons, the Walkers, the Stones, the Johnsons, the Prebbles, the Smiths, the Bradleys.

Then, there was the twenty-year old from the Gates family on Longfellow Street. I decided he was the one I'd marry! Afi I was fifteen, my mother put a stop to my daydreams about this church-going, handsome, fun guy, who pursued me by begging my mother on his knees. It didn't matter what he did or said— she flat out refused to allow him to ever be my friend. Never again would I meet a dashing spark in a man as warm, as tender, as innocent, as promising, engaging or agreeable as this one. I said, never!

Recognizing Oppression

The fall of 1969, I took my beloved sociology at Eastern Michigan University. With a Chinese professor, the course seemed easy and engaging yet again, as I had remembered the course from Mr White in high school. Even though her thick accent made her difficult to understand, I did not see how other students planned to pass the class without ever attending. Now that I'm a senior citizen, I realize the degree of animosity demonstrated by the white students who failed to attend class or interact during her class discussions. I looked around each class period at an eerily dead silent, scantily attended, cold class. She would be so nervous while she gave her lectures that I still remember her relieved smile when she looked my way and I was following along. Propensity studies, duckling imprint identification, anonymity... I would be the only student answering her questions or dialoging with her. At the time, it seemed like such a waste of money for students not to receive her great knowledge. As a teacher, myself, I now understand the methods students can use to make sure a teacher is dismissed.

In my political science class, the main thing I remember is the discussion on how we thought American society could be changed. It was my first time having to defend an opinion. I contributed that, in order to manage a significant change for the better, our country would have to educate. I felt like a lot of students came around to my point of view after thinking about what I was saying.

But during that fall, our friend, Bob, president of the Black Student Association, was put on trial. A new charge was created for him that no one had ever heard of— "Inciting to Riot". Lucky for him, his parents could afford Kenneth Cockerel, a Civil Rights attorney from our home town of Detroit. At that point, it became crystal clear to me that a brush with years in prison over picketing in front of Eastern Michigan University President's house was a contrived problem. The trial had delivered a message to all us Black students sitting in the court room that day. There is a plan against us, corroborated, unfair, unorthodox, secret. Not only would we have to buck up and support Bob—we would always have to support one another, because it could be any number of us charged in the future.

The educational authorities were not only uninterested in our wellbeing on campus, they would use felony charges against us if we complained about our treatment. Internalizing that clear message, I wanted to reject it, but my white roommates were so entitled that I had to accept that the message did mean me. The threat of retribution on campus only underscored how my white roommates from rural Michigan helped themselves to my electric makeup mirror and moving my personal items around.

On the other hand, whenever I used their shampoo, with the label, "for blondes" on it, they challenged me. Before I could even think about it, I raged out and grabbed the nastiest one, with all the mouth, by the neck. I threw her up against the wall and screamed into her face with my fist drawn back. She never spoke to me again, and all that intimidation from those white roommates stopped. The brand new dormitories, Hill and Hoyt at Eastern Michigan University, had dropped me into a foggy, isolated underclass.

Mtengwa

The Aquarian Spiritual Center was located on Santa Barbara in Los Angeles, where the extended University of Southern California is now. Mtengwa led us back to the beginning of human life through the Black Gnostic Studies. The Studies were patterned after the Secret Mystery Societies of ancient Egypt. He presented the archetypal man, the composite of the first human being found in Olduvai Gorge… "the bowels of black Africa, known as the dark continent, that is where human civilization began, where the first human being originated", he taught us. Each Saturday morning, we learned who we were through books and authors we had not known before. Some books we purchased, according to personal interest. We came face to face with who we were before slavery, before Jesus, before Greece. It was me, he meant when he talked straight into our eyes, I thought. I have in me the entire human experience as a black descendant. I am Solomon's love that he tells, "Your breasts are like two fawns", Song of Songs 4:5. Yes, fawns are the exact color of me. Those ancient groups, before the Old Testament, mentioned in the Bible, are me. I am of Cush and the Sabeans, in the Old Testament, before Europe claimed the Egyptian Hebrews. Empowered, I read and understood. Through symbols revealed in my dreams, I was promoted to Neophyte. I had no idea that the directions to life were transmitted by detailed symbols in dreams. Stimulating the conscious mind allows energies that carry information to be laid bare more quietly and quickly. How ancient people learned is carried in the mysterious building of the pyramids in Africa and on their walls. The brain can function in ways that European education does not stimulate. There in the Aquarian Center, we focused on brain sections that common schools do not use. If the brain is not stimulated, much sensitivity, especially in the arts, is lost.

Life's incidents are more connected, purposeful, intentional with a general theme: tied together by what is referred to by esotericists as the Silver Thread. As a child, visiting the Museum of History in Chicago, I noticed a vast number of urns in the exhibit. It was explained that each organ of the body was preserved in an urn when individuals died. As an adult, reading the book of Jeremiah, chapter 31:33 in the Bible, I remembered the value placed on each organ in Ancient Egypt. The Exodus from Egypt brought those people of Israel and of Judah into a new covenant with their Lord, letting them understand how the spiritual communication would go. The verse reads, as God speaks about them, "I will put my law in their minds and write it on their hearts. I will be their God and they will be my people." Hebrews 8:10. Visit online, on "YouTube:

"The Dogon Tribe-Hidden"

"Sacred Geometry"

"The Scientific Method of Inquiry"

"Spiritual Secrets of the Carbon Atom", Shri Mataji, (gathered from YouTube 2015)

"History of Science", Dr. Kerry M

"Introduction to Kemet"

"Kemet and Maat: before Judaism, Christianity and Islam"

"Don't Miss! The Secrets Hidden in the Pyramids of Egypt"

"Cosmological Symbols"

"San Bushmen of the Kalahari", Jenni Siri, (gathered in 2015)

"Hidden Figures trailer: NASA's overlooked black female mathematicians"

It was here that I first learned of The Stolen Legacy, by George G. M. James (YouTube: "Stolen Legacy"). I would learn about the expedition of the archeologist, Dr Leaky, who, with his family, traversed east Africa and discovered the very first human existence. Today, his discovery is validated by the melanin element of the human body, which can be traced geographically, as well as through artifacts, and human migration patterns out of Olduvai Gorge, Tanganyika. Lucy, the fossil found in Ethiopia is 3.2 million years old, suggesting the possibility that Africans traversed a close area before leaving a more widespread trail of deoxyribonucleic acid as perfect evidence.

I learned that the word "Negro" is a Spanish derivative from the word Niger, which followed the kidnapped from that African area in the 1600s to the Caribbean Islands and South America.

Among these tidbits, I began to assemble what happened to the commonwealths and trade routes across northern Africa. They were studied and pounced upon by European usurpers. Through an elaborate plan, Greece stole and claimed the entire existence of civilizations that preceded theirs. One way to look at ancient Africa is to combine the stories, migration, repatriation, historical religions, customs, artifacts, wars, and

DNA. The consuming web of human relationships was as astounding then as it is today.

I came to realize that this type of theft is what had happened to the kidnapped Africans who were dispossessed, and claimed or bartered and sold as worker slaves in the United States. Clearly, a new group had been created in the Americas. It was possible through rape, secrecy and isolation. It was the exact strategy the Greeks had used on the African continent to usurp their identity, wealth, power and trade with China and India.

The entire ancient knowledge was preserved by those who had studied in the Mystery System in ancient Africa. Their educational dogma is still evidenced on the few remaining obelisks, gates, tombs and pyramids today. Atomic structures, mathematical formulae, philosophical riddles are spelled out, but only interpreted with a trained, artistically, spiritually and intellectually balanced mind. Modern society has compartmentalized learning which renders distinct parts of the mind dysfunctional. This skewed thinking is a great target to be easily manipulated into submission as the Greeks found.

The Greeks labeled all those who had left Greece for their self-discovery journey to Egyptian and Ethiopian universities, all those wise philosophers, as heretics, criminals, lunatics and treasonists. They were outlawed, but among themselves, they had memorized and written all the information of the African secret societies. Traces of these fraternal structures remain identifiable in current societies in Greek fraternities and sororities, masonic orders, Christian religious churches, Jewish circumcision and health regimens, law enforcement brotherhoods and other social organizations.

Hippocrates, Socrates, Aristotle, Pythagoras and Democritus hid away in secret to avoid persecution. But as they were found, they were run out of the country or killed. As soon as Jesus began teaching at 33 years of age, he too was harassed and killed. His mother, a black African, defended the birth circumstances of her son, and his maternal birthright to be educated in his maternal home nation among the nobility.

Just 100 years before his birth, Herodotus writes of the ancient Egyptians, that they are "black skinned and curly haired". Homer writes,

"Of visage solemn, sad, but sable hue,

Short, wooly curls, o'erfleeced his bending head…

Eurybates, in whose large soul alone,

Ulysses viewed an image of his won"

Ancient Asians, with whom African commonwealths vigorously traded, wrote about the powerful, just and beautiful Blacks. 8,000 years before Jesus Christ, Kashta, an Ethiopian monarchy, had conquered Egypt. Biblical history only goes back a couple thousand years before Jesus Christ. Scientific research confirms that there is much more to history; many more contributors, many times more millennia.

Starting with the Greeks, African world domination began to topple. The Egyptian Empire, vibrant before Ghana and Songhai, spread around the Mediterranean, from Italy, through Syria and Asia Minor, down to all of northern Africa from east to west. The Chaldeans, Greeks and Persians were among recipients of the unwritten Secret Mystery System of education. The Greeks spent their time fighting each other and fending off the warring Persians, who finally did conquer them. When Alexander the Great pillaged Alexandria and Timbuktu, he authorized Aristotle to counterfeit and plagiarize all that he could before the books and records were burned. At least an eight-thousand-year Black legacy was annihilated and transported off to Greece between 600 and about 300 BC.

Rome sent Mark Antony to marry Cleopatra, which gave him dominion over all north Africa. Ethiopia lost its power in the 5th century, when Christianity was shifted away from the Coptics. Christianity was imported to Europe as Catholicism. It was laden with pagan practices that do not reflect the directives of Christ. Europe began to recognize the advantage in accepting the Greek philosophers. Immediately, they waged a pillage throughout Africa to destroy schools, universities, religion, paintings, buildings, statues, towers, bridges, farms, tools, water supplies, stores, factories, hospitals, and especially libraries. They hailed Greece as the first human civilization.

Just a few years later, African women were taken over by Muslims, just as is happening in modern Nigeria in current times. Through these women's babies, Islam is spread and kept alive. Its founder, Mohammed, called for obedience of slaves to masters. What a convenient brew to justify more domination of these ancient Jews. This group of blacks had been freed from the Pharaohs of Egypt, and managed to fight their way down to west Africa for a bit of peace, only to have been trapped again by their religious role of slave. These Israelites had also been tracked by the books of the Bible, which indicated that they were God's people, but just could not seem to keep their covenant for righteous behavior.

While I was in Los Angeles, I visited the Manly P. Hall Center. It housed an extensive Egyptology department. People were trying to unravel hieroglyphic characters, intent on what these ancient Africans were trying to convey. The massiveness of the display spoke out to the imagination. How many blocks or miles must the legacy of knowledge have been that was destroyed under Alexander the Great!

I remember the paintings left, that showed hundreds of people with the skin colors, from white albinos to tar black people. Such orderly arrangements that the idea of government, family, employment came to mind. While kicking around Turkey from 1984 to 1986, I was privy to much more than the white military and their families. My dark-skinned family was preferred in shops, transportation, restaurants, travels and formal invitations with no apologies to the whites.

Speaking Turkish or Arabic, it seemed important for them to express to us that we were being taken to heart by the Arabs. They made sure we saw the blue-black paintings of Mother Mary and Jesus, and that we saw the Hittite sculpture and paintings. They insisted we see the kinky, coiled hair and the enormous noses of the Hittites. Later, when I was contemplating back, they may have thought my father and I were direct descendants of these precious antecedents.

In the cities, Arabs would always approach me, speaking Arabic to me, taking my hand in theirs to walk a few paces. Smiles showered upon me, hot chai to drink with extra cubes of sugar. All the families showed me off whenever I came into Adana, where they'd force feed me until I'd be ready to throw up. They wanted me and my family to know their holidays, their candies, desserts, bakeries, street vendors, hair products, soaps, perfumes, lotions and their national leader, Ataturk.

The men recognized my son, named after black King Ramses, and showed him extra bits of attention and kindness. He'd be pulled out of line at stores to be first, and taught how to move the pieces in the game of Tavala, while sipping Coke. They were so proud of him approaching manhood in their midst.

We were at ease traveling into the city, while the white women matched scoffs between themselves and the darker skinned Turks. I was a little embarrassed for the white ladies when we attended a makeup class given by a Turkish woman at the base department store. Sitting in the makeup department, the woman commented on how badly the white women needed a lot of makeup. "You can see right through your skin to those ugly green veins!"

I was so surprised when I visited Cameroon and Equatorial Guinea on west Africa's coast that I found all these same colors of people that I had not seen elsewhere in the world. All these naturally blonde kids, what we call redheads with very light eyes buzzed around together with no regard to color. It let me know that the migration from this continent brought most of these characteristics with them when the various racial groups were created.

My brother had understood the same message at San Bernardino Valley College in California. Consequently, he invited me to Los Angeles to study with him under Dr Alfred Ligon at the book store he owned. We both knew we had to find a way to rise above being targeted. I had saved enough money from my secretary job at Anderson Pipe Fitting, down the street, for the two day bus ride across America. On a bright California Saturday morning, in March 1970, I met Dr Ligon and his wife, Bernice.

He was a stern, no-nonsense leader, who could look at us and know all about us, but gave us the dignity of a personal horoscope reading. Each person introduced to the Esoteric Black Gnostic Studies discovered their "unction", a term to describe our purpose on earth. He was careful to recruit us, young, intellectual minds to cultivate. He endeavored to free us from the doubt instilled by an indoctrinating school and church system by reinventing our self-perception. A much larger volume of information was presented for our consumption than what the universities required. The Aquarian Spiritual Center put a screeching halt to all the acts of white supremacy we had endured growing up.

We turned our hair natural, replaced the label Negro for Black, donned African dashikis, jewelry, head and body wraps. We filled in our missing history with ourselves, the archetypal man. We'd have to learn our spiritual heritage, in order to sidestep the traps laid down by Willie Lynch's "kit".

Come to find out, this was the oldest and largest Black-owned book store in the United States. While we were students there, the label Negro was removed from our ethnic group. According to musical artist, James Brown, "I'm Black and I'm proud" should be the mantra springing from our hearts and minds. If we had never known change and hard work before, we learned it from Alfred Ligon. He told us how he would walk miles when he didn't have enough car fare, how he saved his money for twenty years as a porter on the trains to open the Aquarian Book Store. Discipline and focus would be how we would overcome those invisible chains absorbing our mental energy.

Most of what I learned from Dr Ligon came through his ability to intimate. He said teaching is bringing out of the seed, what lies dormant inside the seed. He presented the yogas, psychic abilities, self-talk and dream symbol interpretation as part of a regimen to recreate our higher selves. It was through these and more esoteric studies, and not mainly through the intellect that he reached into our deeper existence, using the learning format of the ancient priests of Kemet; before it was renamed Egypt. We all learned more from him than we had in college. None of us would possess our ability to access our unction if not for Brother Ligon.

Because of YouTube, most of what he taught us can be viewed in current videos.

1. "Spiritual Secrets of the Carbon Atom"
2. "The Secrets Hidden in the Pyramids of Egypt"
3. "Kemet and Maat: Before Judaism, Christianity and Islam"
4. "Destruction of Black Civilization", Dr Chancello Wiliams, Dr John G. Jackson

One of the most impressive of us was a young man named Richard King. He became the leading scholar in the world for the melanin studies. Frequently referred to as the "Black Dot Theory", he cross references the verification of man's ability to achieve other civilizations as developed as this one today.

After viewing this on YouTube, (Dr. Richard King's "Black Dot Theory") please answer the following two questions if you are taking the course:

1. What is the Black Dot Theory?
2. What abilities does melanin contribute to the body?

Education is Political

Eleven colleges and universities; Momma told me getting higher education would speak for me when I applied for jobs. Doctor's offices would laugh out loud, hospitals would just blankly stare when I applied. A brand new suburban hospital in Michigan told me I needed a license after I graduated from Wayne County Community College as a medical laboratory technician in 1975. The white lab tech they picked to show me around, I knew from high school. She told me she had not been to college, nor had she gotten a license. The hospital trained her.

After graduating Michigan State, I applied in one of their labs. After no jobs requiring a Bachelor's degree ever responded to my 100 resumes with my picture at the top, I figured out that the professor did not mean me when he had instructed the class to print our pictures on the resume. At the lab interview, the director peaked her head around the corner, looked at me and never came back. I waited over an hour before being told the director was not in.

Michigan State did not list me as a graduate. They claimed my three-year-old and five-year-old had damaged the apartment at $1,500 worth. My mother knew we had not broken out the windows and knocked holes in the walls. She took a $1,500 check 75 miles to satisfy that lie so I could get transcript copies for employment. Thirty years later, the President of Michigan State publicly apologized, and finally recognized me and several other Blacks and women as alumni. I would feel a glum resentment whenever I'd seen alumni publications that the white graduates were receiving, but I wasn't.

After graduation, in 1979, I followed my boyfriend to West Palm Beach, Florida, on an employment offer from his father, very successful in office machine sales. I discovered that I couldn't make heads or tails of what to do in sales, so I fell back on my laboratory skills. The slow Black staff at the clinic where I began to work would stare at me, and the supervisor was constantly butting into my work, quizzing me on everything I knew. When I went down in the basement one day to recover some supplies, the Black workers cornered me to talk. They said, as long as the clinic had been open, no Black person had ever worked on the floor above the basement.

The clinic could use me as their race and gender compliance with the law, but in a couple of weeks, even that was over. At that white clinic, my supervisor told me I was being let go because a doctor's son wanted my job.

I never got a chance to use that Urban Development degree from Michigan State, but I had a family to feed. Mrs Hay, a Floridian, knew from how her son, Bernard, returning back home addicted to pain killing drugs, that I may never get to use my degree for anything but the traditional job of teaching in Black schools. This insight prompted her to continually encourage me to apply to Palm Beach Schools.

Bernard and I had been students at Michigan State together, in the College of Urban Development. That college could boast a contingent of the best Black professors in the country. They had turned the study of race injustice inside out, putting it to the numbers. Their research and statistics painted for us a clear and decisive portrayal of Black American disenfranchisement.

As a battered football player, Bertram Bernard Hay got me hired by the university to tutor himself and his teammates through academic studies. I kept them eligible to play his nose guard and other defensive positions. He did get drafted by the Denver Broncos, and several others went to the Cleveland Browns or elsewhere. His parents were so grateful that they invited me to live at their Florida home while pursuing my first graduate employment. But his mother grieved that Bernard was cut from the Broncos and had no job prospects in Florida. He'd always express his shame after interviews that no company would hire a man of his dark color.

With two children to feed, I had to quickly get paid, so I listened to Mrs Hay, Bernard's mother, when she said to go to the school board. Sure enough, I was on schedule with the next pay check to feed my kids. She and his father seemed to make the connection between me keeping their son academically eligible to play football while we were at Michigan State University, and being loyal to my escape from being singled out to lose my lab job in segregated Florida. In fact, she knew these segregated schools had not prepared Bernard properly to go through college anyway.

Teaching at Roosevelt Middle School, nobody ever warned me to pull the shades down and shut the lights off when I heard shots fired in the alley. I think my supervisor should have mentioned it when he shut off the classical music I had playing for the kids while they worked. Otherwise, they'd chatter, aimlessly roam the room, steal, fight, tear down the bulletin board, write in the books or on the desk…maybe even leave! Worse yet, they'd curse each other out for the pure entertainment of it.

I learned that schools named after presidents or Martin Luther King Jr. would be in poor, violent, ragged neighborhoods. I learned that sadness was what they were responding to. I had to assign a rude and crude 8th grade girl to after school detention, because she was disruptive and never did any work either. She refused to sit down at detention and abruptly told me she had to go. She had a baby at home.

A shabby, mute boy was brought to class by the counselor late one morning, needing a bath, haircut and some clean clothing. He was fifteen years old in this 8th grade science class. The counselor told me he had been abandoned and lived in a homeless group of older men on the streets. He'd been homeless for years, and that's how he had lost the ability to speak. His name was Collie; yeah, like the dog.

When the school semester was over in Florida, my grandmother had died. I returned home to Michigan for her funeral. A stroll with my mother in the woods behind our summer home brought us upon our neighbor, Mrs Looney. She was so excited that her grandson, Butch was coming home, too. She told us he always wanted children, but his wife had just died. She would make sure he called me in a few days.

It was exciting for Butch and I to reconnect. How adventurous I found his Air Force life when he came to my parents' Detroit house to pick me up. He was extremely thrilled to meet my children. We reminisced about being carefree kids at our lake houses, just waiting to travel the world. He made me a deal for a better life and invited me along with him. So, we packed up and went to Nevada!

On the Strip and downtown, my new husband told me that when he first joined the Air Force in the 60s, Black people had not been allowed to walk the Strip. The only jobs I noticed Blacks doing in all Las Vegas was behind the scenes in the kitchens, with the garbage or handling baggage.

Butch began coming home from duty at the base complaining about being squeezed on the job, and wondered what to do. He was due to retire in just three years. Also, at Fay Herron Elementary, our son Ramsey had begun to be harassed and labeled by his teacher. I said, "Let's relocate!"

When we stepped off the plane in February 1984, at Incirlik, Turkey, I had never seen such handsome men in my life. Olive complexions, thick dark silky hair, hazel eyes, unassuming postures, immediate smiles, gentle gestures…Oh, if I had been single, I thought. Were these the terrorists I was supposed to be afraid of? Surely there must have been some mistake. These men gazed at me so tenderly as they helped me down from the plane. They were the most gentle and mannerable men ever. In Turkish, they welcomed us and beckoned us. I had never been so visible or welcomed. Right then, in that instant, is when I confirmed the lifelong suspicion of mine. I had been considered an enemy in the United States, which had carried an unsavory racial motive toward me. Convince me that I had no right to belong, and supposedly, I would compromise all my integrity. What other American lies would be uncovered about my blackness here?

There were independent contractors working here. The Black ones and their wives were very distraught, complaining that the wives were never hired to work, but white wives were. Obviously, when white wives left the base at the end of the assignment, they had great down payments for new homes. Particularly inflammatory was that, as military wives, these Black women had also suffered the same discrimination in employment while accompanying their husbands. Young, twentyish white girls were treated like royalty overseas, but these Black women huddled together, unincorporated into the mainstream American social setting. Bitterness prevailed.

My husband settled our family into Turkish life. He treated the Turkish co-workers with dignity and respect. They in turn invited us into their homes and events, cheering our presence.

Cheering our presence on the base also was Ms Hallekci. She was my son's 4th grade teacher from Germany. Treating my son as human instead of by Black code, she enjoyed teaching him as much as he could learn. That school year, she sent for us to say that Ramsey had completed the whole 4th grade and the whole 5th grade. She wanted him double promoted. And that, he was.

But bitterness prevails in my heart when I have to remember how the Air Force child care center allowed my children to go outside to play unsupervised. One was kidnapped. During and after that tragedy, the Air Force never provided a stitch of service to our family. The Turks did…

My kidnapped child and I have concluded that our lives were not valued as they should have been. When I almost drowned in the Mediterranean Sea, a German swimmer swam out to get me. The white Americans had sat far or left when we approached the beach to swim. The few available individuals that were scattered on the warm beach sand helped to pull me up out of the sea water. A medical doctor ran over to me immediately, falling to his knees to take my pulse. Pronouncing that there was no pulse caused the white American soldiers to cluster about my lifeless body. I could hear them chattering about how to free my lungs of water, but I couldn't make them hear me talking back to them through a mouth that would not move. I could also hear my husband crying and screaming, "She's dead, she's dead!" A couple of soldiers corralled him while two of them began grabbing, pushing and rolling me, while beating on my back. Suddenly, one of them picked me upside down into the air while the other continued beating on my back. Working as fast as they could, the sand and water dislodged from my throat, unplugging my nose and ears. I gasped, and more water shot out my silenced mouth.

The sea shrunk back from a roaring monster that had controlled me into a quiet, calm-looking glitter in the evening sun. I stared back at it in frozen fear my whole body, shivering. What a liar it had been to force itself down my unsuspecting throat, knock me into rocks, suck my head below its fierce waves so that I could not breathe or move against the swirling pounds of water on my own! Intense anger vowed me to never forget the raging power of the sea.

Not able to speak for hours that evening, I didn't realise this was what people call a near death experience. I remember getting outside of myself, while I dressed up in my new black strapless bathing suit, with the hot pink water lily on the side. It was too late to take a swim, but my husband eagerly joined me when he saw me leaving our beach nestled hotel room door. Nothing felt right, even when he caught me by the hand to skip in the waves with him. He had held on tightly when he felt me step into a hole, created by an under tow. Next to his firmly planted feet, his instructions followed in his demanding voice. "Come back!" The sucking of the undertow was so strong, that I gave up fighting. "Swim!" he yelled.

When I yelled back, "I can't!', he began swimming towards me. The last time I surfaced from the overwhelming waves, I yelled back, "Don't come out here. You'll drown!" I was terrified as I began a desperate prayer. I had begun a freefall through a foreboding darkness when I said, "Oh God." As quickly as a finger snap the entire fall, the fear, the pressure of the water, the cold, the whole struggle halted and an authoritative voice spoke directly to me, accompanied by a blinding light the power of which I have never known in this world before.

It said, "Don't be afraid! Two divers or a boat will come for you when I'm done talking! I had to bring you out here because you don't listen. There will be another Civil Rights Movement in the United States, which you must be a part of. You have to go back there." The voice began to explain the workings of all of creation in which I belong for just seconds until, as if in a dream, I felt a tugging on my feet and arms. It was the divers.

Shirley and Bill Hayes, two Baha'i friends I met at our next duty station in Las Vegas composed my story with others, which they heard. It was only then, so many miles away from Turkey, that I realigned that what I experienced was commonly referred to as a near death experience.

A few of the white wives took me to their rooms to hot shower me, but after that, never spoke to me again.

We were glad to get home, but the difference in our treatment between the Americans, the Turks and other foreign nationals was tremendously apparent.

In Turkey, I was able to perceive how right Mrs. Hay had been about the white establishment only allowing me to use my BA degree for teaching. When we got back to Las Vegas, an older 6th grade teacher, Mrs Stephens taught Ramsey's class. As a Black educator from Ohio, she too seemed to accept that most Black college graduates taught. She offered to help me, and told me just how to acquire my first teaching certificate. I needed more education credits from University of Nevada Las Vegas, for a Substitute Credential.

A veteran teacher from Chicago complained to me when we signed up for the Nevada Writing Project through University of Nevada Las Vegas. Her principal had humiliated her by saying her braided hair was not professional enough. The managing professor of our writing class, she indicated, had also not supported her research on English Language Immersion. She chose me as her friend and confidante that summer. The white teachers in the program ignored us both, while the white professor aggrandized their writing styles and projects.

Simple, to describe their writing about the Oregon Trail. No paper treated the circumstances of slave ancestors or Native ancestors who were not on that Trail experience. Mine was the only story that focused on what I knew my slave and Native relatives were doing next to the Trail, while the whites traveled West. The class went dead silent during my turn to share my story of the Oregon Trail. I found I had to submit to the class that maybe we should consider comparing excellence in creative writing with the rest of the world, instead of a small American subset. The professor and the students looked blank and quickly turned away. My suspicion that the Writing Project was purposely belittling the work of Lorraine and me were verified as educational articles began to spring up praising English Language Immersion as the latest greatest strategy!

I quickly dropped the comprehensive social studies credential assigned by the State of Nevada. I knew I would have to, after the elementary education supervisor at University of Nevada told me to go back where I came from instead of enrolling in their School of Elementary Education.

On the elevator, up to the Secondary Education Office, I schemed about how I could seem like a pacifist in order to get enrolled in the Secondary School of Education. For sure, the whole staff was completely different from the elementary department. They were interested in me enough to document what I needed to receive a secondary teaching credential. If I had believed that first administrator, I never would have witnessed the difference in how I was treated on the floor above the Elementary Education Office. With a teaching major in both social Studies and the sciences, I'd teach kids the truth about science which could never be misconstrued or lied about.

University of California San Diego, the last University, was my best experience because they never saw my face. I could not understand why I was so reluctant to say anything distasteful about any of my childhood teachers. An essay question on which we were to write was the discrimination we endured in school. I truly did not remember any at that moment, so presented my teachers as some saints! I was offended that anyone would have the nerve to accuse my teachers whom I loved with all my heart. As a child, I must conclude that my innocence was my shield against instances I can now see were just plain wrong. I was so unaffected because I was unable to conceptualize racism then. Just as Black American chattle slaves had no comparison to being treated any other way, I had no idea that I should be suspicious of those teachers. If anything, I thought of them as uninformed…which was not half wrong.

It made me very anxious when I did go into education as a career, to find the teaching and learning standards so low. As though it was a scene from the "kit", African American students were succeeding in sabotaging their own education at school. Teaching the sciences, I became a particular target for students, who didn't want to buckle down, and administrators, who didn't want to see Blacks in science fields anyway.

My first year of teaching was no different than my last year, thirty-five years later. Even though I had an Associate of Science degree, a Bachelor's degree in social studies and a teaching credential in both, I was always placed in low-achieving schools. From Florida, to Nevada, Michigan, Massachusetts, California, overseas, privately or publicly I was accused each year of random accusations that made no sense.

In 2001, the Oakland, California High School where I was teaching asked me to do a lesson on the 9-11 bombings. I had not said a thing when it happened, because it was too controversial for me, a recent visitor to the Middle East. My family was usually mistaken for Arabs, so our reception was very sweet. Unfairly singled out, my lesson was on not worrying about being targeted. African Americans do not need to be afraid of people who understand our plight. They are fighting the same unfairness as we are. Just use this time of confusion to buckle down and read. In a matter of weeks, I was being investigated. After I had spent the summer taking another course in space science and writing curriculum from the California State Science Standards for the school district, I was being accused of not knowing facts. The science superintendent and a staff lawyer entered my class while I was teaching and rummaged through my desk. In a few more weeks, I asked for heat in the class for my students because we could see our breath in the air. By the end of October 2001, the principal interrupted my class with an envelope while I was talking to the class. It was a release from service.

Of course, I wrote a federal complaint, also naming the district's superintendent, Mr. Chaconnes for not investigating, since I had been recruited from Massachusetts not even 90 days ago. Promised relocation expenses, I was not even offered teacher housing like all the other recruited teachers from the Philippines. Neither, the Teachers' Union, nor Federal Government mounted any action on my behalf.

The other African educators in Alameda County began meeting with me at the NAACP office. By the time school was over that year, all of them had been dropped from their positions, as well. One vocal teacher's house mysteriously burned down. One teacher suffered from nervous shock and retired early. Three teachers died of heart attacks. The first one released, biology teacher and medical doctor Omubu, from Nigeria, became severely depressed. Four more retired early due to the pressure.

I was so ashamed at what had happened to me, I never knew the fate of all the others. A cheerleader of mine, Mr Reeder, the social studies teacher called a football teammate of his, one town over. He let me come work on a short contract to end the school year.

A big white boy in the health class I was teaching sketched the big tree in front of the school, with a noose hanging from it. I reported him to the principal, who did not see any alarm or offense in it. It had been an intimidating symbol when I was a child of certain death promised to any Black person in the American south. Called, "Strange Fruit", Billie Holiday sang about the horror of lynchings in the 1940s.

I tried to get away as soon as possible, home…to West Africa. In the air, the whole social climate and food changed on that airplane. Real cream and butter, homemade bread served with a real coffee. Nothing tasted artificial.

The first group of African women that welcomed me in a meeting of Baha'is made me lose my composure. I sniffed back my tears as I noticed the dignity of these women that I had never seen or ever felt myself. Cameroon put the missing component of me back into my soul. Eru from the woods became my favorite food, and the women became my example of what true friendship should feel like.

So many ways my father had, I saw there. Cooking outside, remembering the past, hospitality. All the neighbors served me a meal anytime I entered a home. They knew who I was, and embraced the long years of separation I carried in my heart. The king offered many acres of beautiful land to welcome me, but my kids were still back home. Between two worlds…I couldn't leave them.

But the biggest eye opener did not come from my Black brothers and sisters. It came from Dr Samandari, the Persian doctor. Obeying the Baha'i request to serve the needs of Cameroon, he came with his British wife way back in the 1950s, to befriend the indigenous farmers. In fact, he called them down from the mountains, up from the valleys and many miles away to have them meet me. I couldn't believe he thought I was that important, or that they would really travel to see me.

I will never forget, at over 80 years old, with his wife bedridden, he prepared a lunch with his own feeble hands, insisting that I sit and converse with the visiting women. He demonstrated through me what it meant to be fair. Near the end of their visit, he told them that they should observe how easy it was for me to hear from anyone white and anyone black. With the same fair ear, mixed blood leads to peace. I would side with neither black nor white, but both equally. I had never noticed I had that advantage before.

Even though Mr Devini was a likeable, easy going white man, he didn't seem to get what a hard time I was having staying employed in California schools. He gave a glowing recommendation to Mr Jones at the next high school. From New York, this was a fair minded Black man who rewarded me with a new desk from Office Depot for the work I did for him. He was the most professional leader I had worked under in California. He told the truth about me, but in a few months the district superintendent began pressuring him. I overheard a couple of their conversations when I collected my mail in the office.

It became obvious that it was not only me on the public school chopping block. At the next faculty morning meeting, a charmed staff member heard Mr Jones announce trouble brewing, of which he didn't know the finale. I had heard him ask the superintendent which of his demands should be met first because it was impossible to do them all at once!

After this Black man was demoted, I knew it would get rough. The new principal, Mrs Banchero, was a white gym teacher. She would burst into my class with lies and criticisms, of which students began to snicker. They began to sit and chat, not listen or work. They were written up by me daily, but continued to throw, curse, and horse play all period.

That year, the new vice principal wrote that the chemistry bead model, that I first used at Oakland Community College in Michigan was for 5th graders. Neither she nor the new principal did anything to protect the girls when I had them write down descriptions of how they were forced to sexually respond to the male substitute. He demonstrated how to drop wax from a lit candle onto his body and described some of the female's body parts that aroused him. Upset, I delivered copies of the letters to the principal. I took the originals to the Equal Opportunity Commission Office in Oakland. They looked at me blankly when I submitted them with no comment. I saw that same substitute on campus a few weeks later after the principal had assured me and the girls he would not be back. How could they feel safe coming to school now? I could tell they no longer felt safe to bend over the counter to look through the microscope. The message had clearly been, no matter how insulted or afraid you are, this white man has the right to intimidate and stalk you.

The drop-out rate was soaring. The twenty-five or so Mexican families organized and went to the school board (including the same kids who tore up the room, played their radios and challenged my authority!). Even though I also signed up to speak, I was made to wait, with my nine and ten-year-old foster kids, and until congratulations were given to a school board member and her new wife. Everyone was either gone or packing up to go by the time I got permission to approach the podium to speak. A news reporter noticed all this and asked to interview me.

As the articles came out in Hayward's newspaper, pointing out that I was one of Tennyson High School's few academic Black teachers, my union rep kept encouraging me to leave. Once they decide they don't want you and you don't leave, they will destroy your career. I believed in the legislation against discrimination which saw the end of the Civil Rights Movement. I believed that Americans wanted to get it right and be just.

I was about mid-way through the California system which leads to retirement, so I decided to stay and tough it out. At the middle school I went to in Stockton, it was more of the same. Students refused to come in the classroom door on time. Instructional time was so lost that their grades were mostly failing. I remedied this by calling parents. Of course, parents were mad at me. When I had to report that a boy ran up behind a girl out of seat and enfolded his penis between the cheeks of her behind, I was unable to free her until his grinding had led to his orgasm. They both laughed and none of the kids acted surprised. Everyone was mad at me as though I never should have mentioned it.

At Christmas, I made sure to report each child's behavior in class to their parents. I suggested that no presents be given out. Those parents sounded as exasperated with these children as I was. Surprised, at long last, for their thanks in helping them to discipline their kids, I let the kids know I had formed bonds with their parents. Many of those kids were spoiled by single fathers who didn't know what to do.

The next middle school in Stockton was no different. But the kids did like my space program. The principal objected to them moving about the room to research and build their space crafts. She and a visiting superintendent entered my room and began interrupting this activity by asking them questions of which we had not yet covered. The hands-on part of the project was dismissed by them and the students were browbeaten and directed to sit down. I could see disappointment and resentment building in them and I could feel it burning in me. This administration required me to throw out all the plans I showed at the interview that they had agreed to. The school was using a sit-in-your-seat-boring-worksheet program. The whole faculty was forced into this program.

Administration hated outer space studies. When Jet Propulsion Laboratory in Pasadena, down the freeway from our school, was sending the first vehicle up to Saturn, I let the kids watch it. We were all excited. At that moment, when it landed, we all jumped up out of our seats, shouting for joy! All the scientists on television jumped up, too, slapping hands with each other, hugging, laughing. Our country had done it and it felt like the whole nation was proud. In a few seconds the vice principal came running to the door, screaming at us all to sit down and turn off the TV. "These kids are out of order and I want quiet in here. I want to see you in my office after school," he demanded.

That was where I first heard of Eid, a Muslim holiday he stepped out of federal law to tell me he was celebrating. Obviously, it was his way to take me and the Christian teachers on. I informed him right then and there that I refused the remediation he was remanding me to, like I was a new college graduate with no experience.

He began sending teachers to other schools, writing lies about Christian teachers, processing teachers with tenure to be fired. A whole uproar began among the faculty. I wrote them a letter and challenged them to throw their blue eyes and white skin in the ring to stop this harassment. I happened to run into that same faculty group while leaving Starbucks with two Baha'i friends. The Baha'is were astonished to witness that several of the women from that school ran up to me, threw their arms around me, so happy to see me and report that they did band together. They got rid of that harassing vice principal.

The kids must have begun to feel unstable, because during the California Standard Test they took, I had to begin putting half the class out because of talking, roaming and cheating. One chronically disruptive boy began talking out loud and going up to other students' desks to disrupt them. He was sent home.

When he returned for the makeup test, he came back to me crying. I couldn't believe that he cared about missing it. He sounded a little more mature when he said, "I really wanted to take the test this time so I could see what I know, but it was already filled out!" Looking sullen, he dropped his head. I, just as shocked, became determined to find out what happened.

I couldn't tell him that I had checked in the storage area where the principal and teachers were working to organize all the tests for shipment back to testing headquarters. Very industrious students were sitting around erasing answers and adding new ones from an answer sheet. There was nothing more I needed to ask. This was some of that cheating for which administrators go to jail.

The next day, the principal was absent, so I asked the substitute what could be done for my little one whose test had been filled in while he was absent. He became very interested and wanted the whole story. That was an April afternoon when the regular principal returned. She called me into her office to say, pack up your room and leave by the end of the day. This announcement gave me two hours. Unsure that I would not be breaking the law in a right to work state, I left. She further stated that she was going to make it impossible for me to ever set foot on any school district soil or work at any other school again. I should have challenged her, because records show I had not been fired, rather tricked into leaving.

I began to understand further why poor and Black kids do not engage at school, but I wouldn't give up. The day I began working for California Department of Corrections, I thought for sure it would be justice for all. My first class told me I wouldn't be there long. "You like us," was the reason the 90% Black incarcerated youth told me. Yes, I'd listen to the reasons they were there, and yes, it was for circumstances that adults had placed them in. Who the heck did not understand that any kid would be a runaway if they were being raped? Any kid would steal for food if they had been abandoned in the neighborhood park by addicted parents. Any kid would kill to stop his mother being beaten to death.

Although the law in the union book was posted... recruit, develop, retain and promote employees in the protected classes, none of that protected me. I followed Nancy, my supervisor's instructions to renew my license with San Joaquin County, but they had no authority to issue a new one. She fired me on August 28th before the September 4th credential expiration date. California law also reads that employees have thirty days to correct infractions, which I never got. The court I went to agreed with Nancy, that the due process for which I asked was not meant for me. Even after the State processed my new credential, Nancy merely stated that she did not want me working with her and was granted that wish. White privilege seemed alive and well over the incarcerated boys and over rejected me.

I sat down to my computer in 2008, and banged out one of those Reinvestment project applications President Obama said would create jobs. I was all excited, but nobody in my Black neighborhood trusted it but me. They were gracious and supportive towards me because I was so sure, using all of them as employees in the project. They'd look at me in disbelief; that I believed we would get any Recovery money from Obama. He was Black, so he would make a way for me, wouldn't he? Surely he's cut down the obstacles we'd faced. I got two letters back about my applications, saying I couldn't have financial assistance for my solar energy educational projects.

I had applied in the same batch with Solyndra. They got received three million with three years experience in solar energy. I only asked for a quarter million to educate kids in California about solar energy. Obama reached over me to give this group of newcomers to America a boost instead of me. I, a 3rd generation freed slave, with thirty years of experience in my field, got nothing. Solyndra bankrupted their grant and I wrote Mr President, giving him a piece of my mind!

So, here's when I knew I was done teaching… the first time. At Warren, in Inglewood, California, a group of parents came to see me about how the class was too hard and that I didn't like their kids. Mind you, their kids had all grown up together in that school from first to eighth grade, and come to a crafty set of behaviors. They would begin classes by complaining, moving their seats, not getting out their supplies, laughing, arguing. Wild and undisciplined, they would butt into my first two sentences of the day to say they didn't understand, had to go to the bathroom, were done with the bell work, needed a pencil, that someone teased them, someone stole from them, that they needed the principal. They'd stop all that if the principal would swing by to monitor me. Of course she agreed with all their complaints about me. No, I would begin class anyway by starting the lesson. Oh, you thought they'd settle down, did you?

Well that's when their real antics began. They'd begin yelling out they couldn't see the board, instruction was going too fast, they didn't understand, why do we have to do this…. As the room would get louder and louder, others would begin yelling across the room to their friends, laughing, throwing, going to the waste basket and running around the room. The assignment would still be due at the end of the period, which would leave most of them with a failing grade. In order to cover all this up, they would make up lies about the teacher. It never occurred to the principal to check their work. Parents and administrators were too perplexed by the kids to check why they could not complete some of the work, and let a child's excuse for this be the teacher's fault.

One girl, whose seat had been changed several times for disrupting others sat in front of my face and talked all period, in disregard of any of my directives. I told her I wanted to see her after class. As the other kids were leaving, she screamed at the top of her voice, "I'm going to bring my god damned grandmama up here so she can beat the shit out of your mother fuckin ass, bitch!" Like a prisoner on the countdown, I called the State retirement board to ask how long I had before I could retire. "Oh, two weeks? I'll take it!" I high tailed it out of Warren Lane for retirement, but before I left Inglewood, California, I met with some groups of progressive educators.

The lunch date established with Principal Wisdom from one group of educators tempted me to feel a solution was at hand. She sat calmly, listening to my reinvestment plans under President Obama. A suspicion grew over me at her quiet demeanor, and I realized she had had no intention of collaborating with me to form a new-styled education institution. She left me with her close up observations that verified everything I did not want to believe. The scam was that, administrators knew the best way to ensure steady income to the schools was to keep them failing! They have plenty of schemes to disenfranchise dedicated, good teachers, to make sure they don't succeed with their students. Failing schools get the most money. After all those years I spent making sure to be the most current, best educated, most accurate….it all finally made sense. My mouth fell open when the mystique was removed about why the best teachers had always been the least supported.

In 2010, I remained covered by insurance at UCLA. Getting my blood drawn, a small, pretty, red faced girl approached me, shaking. Her voice wobbled as she told me she was a medical student sent to draw my blood. As she deliberated got the needle ready and applied the tourniquet, her hands were shaking so bad that I stopped her. "Let me help you. Just follow what I say." I walked her through the stick, from which she gathered a luscious group of full test tubes. She was overjoyed with herself and volunteered that this was her very first draw. She is the one who made me promise that I would go back to teach biology. She thanked me profusely for walking her through, and said the kids needed a teacher like me.

But on the first full-time job I accepted in 2015, the principal could not keep out of my room. When it became obvious that he was in there all day every day, he put a camera in there without informing me. Finally, he told me it was in there to watch me because he didn't know what I would do to the kids behind his back. Spying on me was against any law I had ever heard of, such as stalking, discriminating, harassing, targeting. I thought, well, I am a senior citizen, I am Black, I am a woman, I am always the most qualified of all other teachers. Let me allow Jim Elliott Christian High School to reinvent itself.

I had given up on expecting the best from any education system by the time I got to the last one. The biggest room was assigned to me. I came in the door with bags and boxes, ready to unpack and set up for class. The secretary stopped me at the door to inform me of a room change. Another teacher had wanted it, she said. I stopped, threw everything onto an empty table, and answered that I would wait to talk to the assigning principal. I glanced around at how difficult the whole school was for teaching science. No sinks, no ventilation, not enough equipment, junky. To make a quick and easy peace, I cooperated and let the engineering teacher have it, although, after that concession, I never saw her using any materials for which she claimed she needed that room.

In the new room, the principal, Mr Scott, pulled a chair up behind a female student to whisper in her ear. He took her book and left, then came back during a math exercise we were doing on the board as a group. She whispered with him instead of working along with the class. Tongue-in-cheek, I kept on teaching. After class ended, I thought I had better address that he was up on her back like that in case the student needed me to comply with reporting him for sexual abuse.

"I just thought I'd check to understand why you came to my class this morning. I know I was just evaluated in biology, and if you want to use your visit as an evaluation, it's all right. May I sit down?"

He appeared quite indignant as he continued his frowned expression from the visit.

He admitted that he had evaluated me, but not formally. I was anxious to hear what a great job I had done getting all the girls engaged, using prior lessons to substantiate their choice of formulae, and showing enthusiasm challenging each other's applications of formulae. So, I was full of excitement and confidence when I asked what he had found…

"I found you to be incompetent. You look incompetent and like you don't have any confidence. How confident are you in what you're teaching? The students knew more than you. You look like you don't know what you're doing, especially when you were looking for a colored pen to color the graph. I can get plenty of them to say they don't understand the class because it is confusing. Are you following the lesson plan in the book? What does it say to teach? That's not what you were teaching. It never tells you to teach all that math. They don't need all that math for a Chemistry class. Where did you go to college? Have you ever taught this class before?"

I stopped him to redirect his tirade. "I suggest you call Human Resources and set up a meeting to ask all these questions you have. We need to see if I understood something differently from what they wanted. I am teaching this course as a college prep class, because they will be expected to know this math when they take the course in college. OK, let me know when you have the meeting set up for us." Trembling with the anger at the disrespect and personal attack, I couldn't feel compatible with what treachery he would plan for me next. A possible police complaint would leave me unable to work at all. They could shoot me. I snatched some of my things together and headed for Human Resources.

On the phone when I arrived, the District Superintendent threw up a hand gesture that I should wait. I found myself a seat and waited about a half hour, when he barged in the conference room saying he knew all about what happened with Mr Scott. Show me your lesson, he challenged, as if he agreed with Mr Scott's evaluation. In about five minutes, he interrupted to say, "I'm a Harvard graduate of the School of Education and I can't follow your lesson either. It's unclear to me and lacks planning because you don't have a lesson plan." I looked at the Science Department Chair, sitting there, who had my lesson plans, but she never opened her mouth. She agreed with all his far-flung accusations. As he rudely packed up and got up to leave while I was answering, I knew Pacific Charter Institute did not have enough integrity for me to remain. Nobody can make me falsify the science agreement I have with the State of California.

I had explained to the principal that integral to the learning of chemistry, is the state requirement that calculation objectives be met. For the following, I am responsible.

Use the ideal gas law to do calculations

Learn to calculate the concentration of a solution made by a dilution

Learn to do calculation for acid-base reactions

Understand the law of chemical equilibrium and how to calculate values for equilibrium constants

Learn to calculate the solubility product of a salt given its solubility, and vice versa.

What I have presented are only a few. Students usually enter the class unprepared in math, which means extra attention to this part of science is necessary. At Warren Moon, 6th grade teachers were given amnesty when they emphatically admitted their purposeful omission of science from the elementary curriculum. I found lack of math preparation to be typical and a valid reason for student combativeness in the secondary sciences.

Tracing Archetypal Man (I Mean Woman)

I had been right when I presented my high school biology students with "The Real Eve". Eve had lived in Africa, some 150,000 years ago. About 80,000 years ago, the human species roamed off the continent. Stone tools were found had the ash from the volcano eruption of Mount Toba 74,000 years ago. Zaraina Majid, an archaeologist in Malaysia further validates the presence of this group in Malaysia with mitochondrial DNA, which shows them as direct descendants of the African they had left behind 80,000 years prior.

At a 70,000-year interval, the dark skinned, blonde headed aboriginals are related through their DNA right back to the Malaysians. In Australia, these people drew on their cave dwelling walls, showing animals that are now extinct. This migration throughout the world leaves us as a whole unit, regardless of the time that has passed.

What we have evolved into is in our imagination, and has served us well in being able to take advantage of each other. The fact remains that physically we humans all share the same chemical makeup. Our skin color is made mainly of melanin. If an organism does not have any in their skin, they are albino. Melanin deposits can be found throughout any human body in various locations. It colors the eyes, hair, gums. Deposits can be made in the internal organs of the body, as well. If a pair of black-colored parents both have a recessive gene for albinism, they are able to produce a child with no melanin. This child can be white skinned. Some questions beg to be answered: is an albino child born of two Black parents belong to the white race? Are the rules we follow for race identity accurate? What if an albino has as much melanin located in their liver, kidneys, or heart as a Black person has in their skin. Which one is a Negro?

Skin color is the main characteristic we have been using to disenfranchise groups or privilege others. We have used white to mean privilege. But does that mean albinos get extra privileges? Descending down from white means privileges also descends in human society. Great numbers of members of societies believe that this is natural, right, and good to have societies set up this way, until the table turns for social or economic reasons.

What about a Caucasian girl with kinky hair? Should she straighten it to blend with the Caucasian folks better? What about one with big blue eyes, a long straight nose, stick straight hair, full lips and no buttocks... We may chuckle, but race is as haphazard and confusing as this example.

Scientifically, the Bible is more right than we may initially have thought when it refers to descendants of Adam and Eve, or Noah and his family. Our human population does go way back, and has been genetically influenced by floods, climate, language formation, and diet. When groups of humans have not been separated for a long time, everyone begins to look just alike! Splitting us up brings out different gene combinations, which allows us to look like a beautiful flower garden. What our research has emphatically proven is that humans originate from the same stock group. We are like music or a rainbow. We can separate into the scale of single notes, or seven bands of color, or be compiled into plain white light or a single seven note chord.

We do look like chickens and frogs as we progress though stages in utero, though. Some people may think humans used to be those animals. Our evolution has been the cultures we created.

Guess the next three ethnicities from the descriptions of their attire.

1. A boy is short, has blonde hair, a round face, green eyes, bushy eyebrows, sunburns easily. He is wearing a dashiki, sandals, shorts and a cap made of Kinte cloth. He speaks English.

2. A boy is tall, dark brown skin, no hair, brown eyes. He is eating a burrito, and listening to Jose Martinez on his phone. He speaks French and Spanish.

3. A boy is 5 years old, and eating strained corn pudding. His name is Ahmed. He is wearing some jeans, and his long hair is pulled up into a knot on top of his head.

What race or ethnic group is definitely it for the three boys? Hey, what's the consequence for being wrong? Go online to Harvard's IAP survey to find out if you have bias about different groups of humans.

Humans are a single species; always were! So, why we safeguard our minds from most of our documented history on this planet can be for several reasons that I've thought of. It may seem disrespectful to the idea of Jesus, as the founder of the Christian faith. After all, our calendar refers to before his birth and after his death, as if it is the only valid event that touches human existence. For sure, if we consider Moses, there should be more time added. And think about Zoroaster, or the ancient dynasties like Amen Ra, who brought the first idea of one God thousands of years before Jesus. Are we afraid that the human story is the story of all humans, and not just of one group in particular? Are we too comfortable with wanting our modern day social and scientific constructs to feel impenetrable?

Peace and Survival

To mend this present world, we must view the whole spectrum of human existence: from the time we can first have evidence of our existence throughout all earthly events. Tragedies, catastrophes, and climate changes did not curtail our existence. There is a golden thread that runs through the ages, that links all human life.

We evolved physiologically as we evolved in our social thinking. Stigmas we formed against each other as humans have either vanished, or hold on, like the plagues of disease or agricultural desolation over our thousands of years on the earth. There is no event that has severed any group away from any other group, as a species.

As a human group, we have wrestled with similar conflicts, problems, issues, obstacles throughout the ages. Just being human dictates this similarity in things we consider important. Making that disconnect from other human groups for group self-interest has not served us well. A few individuals may prosper, but we are stronger when we acknowledge that we have always had the abilities that make us evolving human beings. Very clearly reiterated in the book of Ecclesiastes 1:9, the continuity among humans through the ages is coined in the statement by the son of King David. "What has been will be again, what has been done will be done again; there is nothing new under the sun."

In elementary school, we learn that humans need food, clothing and shelter to survive. Well, Social Studies get more complicated as we move through our schooling, until we reach classes such as paleontology or anthropology. As scholars, education has a student consider with what evolving humans were concerned and what adjustments they formulated to survive. Recently, our basic needs have been met well enough for us to use our brains to develop opinions and reactions to each other. Perhaps our historic concern with survival techniques continues to underpin our innate survival behaviors in these present times. Anything from the relics of our past can find itself obsolete as we mature as a human race.

Currently, Americans particularly, and other nationals, generally find ourselves very concerned about acquiring and containing resources for particular groups. Much as birds will squawk, flap their wings and challenge each other when too many birds vie for nesting areas, so too do humans. Although there is enough dwelling space on planet Earth, humans display claims to property in close proximity to each other. We will squawk, argue, fight and even kill each other for claims to parking spaces, medical care, hunting or fishing rights, land use rights, money, services, privacy, partners... so many things. We disenfranchise each other, mainly by race, gender, strength, ability, religion or national origin, in order to gain more of what we are fighting over. This human push and pull for survival appears to have been with us always.

It is good to become more conscious of how we think, so that we can allow unnecessary concepts to be replaced or dropped. At the point we are now, where everyone on earth is acquainted, we need to think as a unit of survivors on the planet. Thinking as an individual, or family ,or even group member will not sustain any success of survival anymore. We have to move on to forge behaviors group-wide, nation-wide and world-wide that guarantee the efficacy of planet earth.

I suggest examining our individual social attitudes that we carry around with us. Daily we respond to an inner tape recording of the decisions we have made about each other. We usually have not discussed our perceptions of the world with anyone outside of ourselves. By close association, our emotions and minds have been most strongly influenced by our families.

For example, a child may think it frightening to cross the street while playing in front of the house. That child may grow up to remain afraid to cross the street to play with other kids if the street remains uncrossed. Finally, the conclusion could easily be made that crossing the street is scary, unnecessary, useless. But the question about what lies across the street is never answered. No real or valid statement can be made about the other side if it is never seen.

Often we live without examining our environments, but will leap to impressions which have never been verified. This is a sanctioned behavior by our societies, because it is customary to make sure we survive. Our survival techniques do not always match the reality of our needs. Our present societal structures have accepted behaviors that tell us we are OK as long as we make sure others do not have a chance to catch up. Allowing others to seem unworthy is quite a common technique for human groups to use disenfranchisement, without too much of a disagreement with each group.

For example, my group of two hundred Caucasian, six foot, young, strong males will overtake vessels on the silk trading route in 2000 BC. In 400 AD, the descendants of my group continue overtaking vessels, but also now burn the crops and schools. By 500 A.D, my group has become steeped in what has become customary, to sail out on the Mediterranean to overtake trading vessels and set fires in cities. By the 1500s, my group and I have destabilized the countries on the silk trade route so much that now, we just take what we want and claim ourselves to be heroic. The orientation of my ancient group becomes to return whence they came.

"I will set a sign among them, and I will send some of those who survive to the nations—to Tarshish, to the Lybians and Lydians..." Isaiah 66:24. These black African groups experienced the return of my group that had migrated away from Kenya. Settling in the Caucases Mountains, much of the Silk Route trade had escaped their participation. They fell behind in their development, but carried the feeling of catching up with them as a culture trait, so that we see this group continuing to destroy other cultures and claiming rights to their history. It is a feeling that surfaces around the world, as my group isolates and ignores the definitions of other nations and other cultures.

European Jews are mistaken for the Hebrews released from Egypt. The original Coptic Christians are mistaken for the Catholics and European Christians. The original genetic man is mistaken for the cave man in Europe, and the original forefathers of one god worship in Egypt have been misplaced. Greece has been substituted as the fathers of civilization, which has disconnected the whole world from the continuity of human evolution.

But this disconnect is subtle, so that history can be rewritten to keep disenfranchisements in place. Information omitted keeps mental shackles in place over groups that accept a falsification of their identities and a siphoning of their strength. We are told in Judges 16 that Samson omitted telling Delilah that his hair was his strength. As soon as he told her, she had him subdued by her people.

Within the history of mankind, the human story is pretty consistent. The small tribes of Jews and Gentiles in the northern Africa were depicted in the Bible as warring constantly with each other, for practically the same reasons large nations come up against each other today! As long as African captives were deprived of the historical identity recorded in the Bible, they were easily subdued. To teach them to read would allow them to reclaim themselves and their Jewish Biblical history. It becomes more and more dangerous to the current peace to have groups reclaiming kinships, for the fear of retribution. At the same time, the evolved human capacity to reason ensures a world balance of power.

Nations are bigger, societies are bigger. As a historical painting of social dynamics, one piece of evidence jumps out in Bible stories. People question, and discuss causes and effects. Compared to then, our families function on a type of autopilot, where distractions take us far from home during the day, and disrupt the custom of conversation within the home. Our daily scheduling simply does not supply the kind of time to ponder upon the meaning of life. We live instant lives, with quick simplistic answers to the meaning of life.

Questions that we don't ask are considered rude.

How am I related to people in the Bible?

How do I receive answers to personal questions?

What determines race?

Am I really the race I've been told I am?

What are the real differences between males and females?

Where do the answers come from for all the information on this planet?

What were lost civilizations like?

What are the changes to names of cities and nations before Greece?

How do I feel about other age groups in this world?

How significant is racial difference in the survival of the human race?

Is there enough room for everyone on this planet?

What does peace feel like?

How do I deal with conflict?

Is war necessary?

How can humans grow toward peace?

Should people talk more?

How do I feel when strangers are different from me?

What do I have to lose when encountering associates from a different racial group?

How can I feel how long ago three and a half million years ago is?

Just how much have human beings changed since the oldest fossilized person was alive, some 3.6 million years ago?

What appear to be African artifacts are found in China, and what appear to be Chinese artifacts appear among the Olmec of Mexico. There is a continuity in our physical existence; in our artistic, dietary, fashion expression over millions of years. The search for meaning seems to evolve with us, strongly expressed just a few hundred years ago with the theft of secret information housed among the Africans, from the Fertile Crescent to the Atlantic Ocean. Victor Frankl, German psychiatrist, quickly gleans this aspect of human awareness as he observed the anguish of the Jews within Nazi concentration camps. In his book, *Man's Search for Meaning*, he discovers the one thing that human beings do when facing death is to hold on to whatever gave them meaning in their lives. What gives a person meaning ties them to life on this earth. It is in the very composition of their will. At the point, that everything in a life has been lost, there is no pretense, no lying to one's self.

Survival is the mechanism of keeping one alive under incredibly inhumane circumstances. It revolves around the refreshing power of plants, the love of a relative, the hope that maybe torture or starvation could ever be overcome. Making sense out of senseless suffering and the torture from other humans, as vulnerable and fragile beings as the prisoner were, was the only way a captive could hold on to the hope of life. These twists and turns in the profound management of consciousness, finding what is worth living for, compensations in the mind for all that was lost, were documented as the work of Viktor Frankl, prisoner of the Nazi concentration camps.

Carl G. Jung in his work, *Man and His Symbols*, also cuts to the core of what makes humans struggle to exist. Humans have many links with each other, denoted in symbols that we all have used, which tie us together from our ancient days. He puts forth that "natural' symbols are derived from the unconscious contents of the psyche, and they therefore represent an enormous number of variations on the essential archetypal images. In many cases, they can still be traced back to their archaic roots—i.e. to ideas and images that we meet in the most ancient records and in primitive societies.

According to Jung, it appears as though the unconscious mind is a vast arena of energy or possibility that the conscious mind may pull upon to express humanness. It has always existed in humans, and serves as an invisible thread that links us in our capacity as humans, so that we essentially remain the same. Just as we recognize each other for our common body shape and physical abilities such as speech and sight, we could also recognize ourselves as a three-million-year old species through the symbols we continue to produce. Under the most trying circumstances of isolation from each other, we continue to be linked in this unconscious way.

David Rock, co-founder of the Neuroleadership Institute is an essential figure in understanding the current brain use of unconscious symbols. As current humans research and discover brain function, thinking records from Africa become more meaningful and clear. Both sides of the brain, the artistic and the intellectual, are always engaged, as well as human emotion and the higher nature. For future posterity, the enormous pyramids and temples in Africa show to the world, for all time's sake, how human beings process attributes and functions of the world around them.

David Rock pinpoints a process by which unconscious symbols trigger prethought responses. He says, "Five domains activate either the primary reward or primary threat circuitry of the brain." Status, certainty, autonomy, relatedness and fairness are the core social domains that drive human behavior. He goes on with much detail and clarity when he explains that "knowing these drivers that can cause a threat response enables people to design interactions to minimize threats…knowing about the drivers that can activate a reward response enables people to motivate others more effectively."

From each driver, he outlines a predictable behavior which makes African American males easy targets for violence and murder by a society that has a predetermined set of excuses for murder. The symbolic nature of these interactions exists within perpetrators of violence, and a different set of emotional symbols within the African American citizenry.

When a person does not feel certain, the brain's pattern-recognition machine is unable to predict the near future. When changes in predictability occur because there is a different response to common situations in society for African Americans, a different part of the brain kicks in.

Take for example, out of 500 people at the airport, the Black person is the only one searched. For instance, if five cash registers are open at the grocery store, four of them shut down when a Black customer tries to get in line. Further, if a Black person expects to enter Disneyland because television shows hundreds of white customers going through the entrance gate with a ticket, but the Black person is not allowed in, even with a ticket. Or, if a stewardess is serving drinks in order, but changes the order so that the Black person is served last. The brain draws upon what has happened with others to formulate what is expected. The breaking away from the normal expectation immediately triggers "a more energy-intensive prefrontal cortex to process these moment-to-moment experiences." Even before there is a reaction to the stimuli, the expected pattern has been broken: "…uncertainty generates an error response in the orbital frontal cortex. This takes attention away from one's goals, forcing attention to the error." It is plain to understand that changing predictability for an African American is a societal trigger, which sets these people apart from the group. The subtlety of this practice covers up the aggressive nature of American society toward the African American group. The triggers are preplanned differences in treatment that undermine the full and comfortable participation of African Americans in American society. Similar tactics sometimes affect other protected classes in the United States.

Walking together toward a peaceful society means: "Meeting expectations generates an increase in dopamine levels in the brain, a reward response. Going back to a well know place feels good because the mental maps of the environment can be easily recalled." This is why equal treatment between racial groups is necessary on our walk toward peace.

Modern humans need to recognize that we have a millions year old history on this planet as one species. From the Greeks until now is merely a few thousand years. Tracing the deoxyriboneucleic acid of human cells, we need to broaden our thinking to include how humans migrated throughout Africa, both east and west. As humans migrated outside Africa, we have developed ever so slight physical changes that we still hold onto in a tribal way. We share unconscious tendencies toward common symbology, but share, physically, artifacts left behind by visiting African sailors hundreds of years before Europeans began to organize societies. During the Middle Ages, war was of grave importance to west African societies, as they fought off the Vikings and eventually lost to colonization. We must begin to understand that what we face in creating peace is no different than the peace humans have sought for millions of years. It would behoove the world to consult with the original peoples of Africa about establishing peace, because of the millions of years they spent dwelling on the same endeavor.

Professor Asa Hilliard at Columbia University makes it clear that after the society of Kmt (Kemet), humans were interested in the virtue of the human self. Their sacred commandments remain necessary, and similar for human reference in the Ten Commandments of the Bible thousands of years later. As the Greeks destroyed most of the ancient African human faces on statues, the postulates for peace among humans did not change for posterity. When I met Asa Hilliard at the Las Vegas Association of Black School Educators conference in 1986, he agreed that public education was missing ingredients that would shape the integrity of students.

King Solomon is one example of having to contend with war, while ruling the easternmost empire of the African dominion, later known as the Middle East. This group of Israelites raised up Solomon's temple in the constructed fashion of one in Timbuktu in Mali.

The Kit

Human symbol speak has rendered us confused about how we should regard one another. This confusion has led us to continually find ways to harm one another. Our unconscious recollection of ourselves as one species is in a state of chaos. This confusion greatly hinges upon chunks of time missing between 3.6 million years ago and now. We learn very little in school about sustained human development for that 3.6 million years ago. We will refer to it as lost. The chaos allows us to conjure feelings that lead us to behave like lower animal species. One of the main repositories of using a new unconscious symbol construct was the "Willie Lynch letter: The Making of a Slave". Since the brain has a system of instant reflex, outside the realm of conscious response to the environment, the reflex system was put to fabulous use by the societal symbols created by Willie Lynch. A host of various symbols taught to a human being will elicit a reflex response, attended by chemical production in the brain. In short, a person's social responses can be conditioned by controlling the social symbols in their life. They can be conditioned to be happy, sad, angry, by being subjected to emotional images.

For example, if tall white men always beat a person, fear will prevail when the person encounters a tall white man, whether being beaten or not. The symbol can be so strong that the symbol of fear can be handed down through generations. Lynch saw the connection of humans from before Christ, and uses their treatment of slaves as a model for his own. He refers to the Bible to shorten the connection between himself and thousands of years ago (This connection was forbidden to black slaves in America, by killing them if they learned to read). He knew his control methods were mental and would "control the slaves for at least 300 years". His drivers were "fear, distrust and envy, for control purposes".

Self-destruction would become the goal for slaves and their posterity forever.

These same *drivers,* as emotional symbols, keep slaves emotionally unsteady, unsure, and unsafe, when they are used against the progeny of slaves today. When these symbols are used, the same reflexive responses based on fear, uncertainty, distrust, and anxiety set the African American apart from the rest of Americans. This *apartness* is approved for the same murder by police as by slavers. Public cries for retraining of police, then, becomes a civilizing goal of the general public.

Hearing answers to questions, verifying these answers is a start away from non-violence. The general public also needs a standard response to police by becoming immobile, less verbal and less challenging. By and large, police becomes slavers, dressed in a uniform. When they have the authority not to follow a strict line of questioning and explanation to their individuals being investigated, they should not expect strict responses.

Questions inform responses. Enough commands and directions have to be given by police, before a stopped individual can process what is being expected of him or her to do next.

How they each process a threat is so culturally different that it winds up in too much death. The brain reflexively processes the "foe" response for all individuals, based on personal experience where emotions have symbolized the "foe" before.

The Willie Lynch "kit" is still being used by police officers, as it was used on plantations by overseers. Lynch declares that it is "your keys to control".

Dismantled human beings remain acceptable today, as the protocol of Lynch is still practiced. "Both horse and niggers are no good to the economy in the wild or natural state. Both must be broken…". In the natural state, a horse and a slave would be looking for the natural state of freedom and will rebel against containment. The expectation of freedom is what makes them dangerous enough to kill a slaver. Slave quarters were established then; ghettos are established now.

The particular focus was to indoctrinate the female slave, that she had no way to take care of her offspring; therefore, it would never belong to her. "…her normal female protective tendencies will have been lost in the original breaking process."

African American women need to be reeducated about who is responsible for their children, and what these expectations look like. How will society restore them back to womanhood and motherhood?

Lynch only loses one male in his economic blueprint to contain slave males for work. He seldom loses a female using the elements of his "kit"…

Take the meanest and most restless nigger, strip him

of his clothes in front of the remaining niggers, the female,
and the nigger infant, tar and feather him, tie each leg to
a different horse faced in opposite directions, set him afire,
and beat both horses to pull him apart in front of the remaining
niggers.

We reversed nature by burning and pulling a civilized nigger
apart
and bullwhipping the other to the point of death, all in her
presence.
In this frozen psychological state of independence, she will
raise her
male and female offspring in reversed roles…for fear of the
young man's life…

Now tell me, how does a civilized nation atone for this savage, violent terrorism against their ever-present progeny of the slave quarters? After, over 300 years, African American women remain the head of household in most Black families. She is 60% more likely to be the sole bread winner, and 90% more likely to be raising her children without their father. She receives the least medical care than any other group, earns less, and is the likeliest to earn far less income than is commensurate with her education.

When the nation of Black sons witnesses this, he is compelled not to respect the design of his birth nation. He flails in order to right these wrongs against his mother, but if he exhibits his natural state of malehood, he is exterminated.

For example, our nation of ex-slaves suffered from childhood poverty and hunger in the 1960s. A benevolent group came together to demand better food and more accessibility to food supplies for Black families. They were angered and demanded: "Black control of the Black community!" The most salient human violation was the indoctrination in public schools to devalue Black students. Coming to school without breakfast made this group of advocates start the Free Breakfast Program. Even though Willie Lynch's containment plan dissolved all Black control of any human existence, these young men and women were systematically exterminated for speaking about changing that animal state of existence. In front of the whole nation, these kids were mass murdered in the middle of the night. There was no public outcry.

The victory of free breakfast and Black history in public education is that African Americans were more visible and more included in the life of the nation. Conflict is ages old, and rests on the same psychological drivers in ancient humans as in modern era humans. We can merely decide to prize peace, or we can repeat the wars, skirmishes and unrest found in the Bible. The fact that humans still roam the earth is a good sign that we can conquer bullying, fighting, maligning, demeaning, depriving, and so many ills that lead to destruction.

The cultural symbols, to which Carl Jung refers, are embedded in the Willie Lynch letter. Most of the stolen Africans were deposited in Central and South America. As a human was masterfully smashed into a slave there, Lynch had time to rethink what those kidnappers should have done to ensure a more effective system. He was at a great advantage while counseling North American slavers in 1712.

Commission, the number of well-dressed, well-educated, well-spoken African Americans are filing discrimination complaints there? Progress has to made in the effort to dismantle Lynch's language part of his "kit". He says, "…if you take a slave, if you teach him all about your language, he will know all your secrets, and he is then no more a slave, for you can't fool him any longer, and being a fool is one of the basic ingredients of any incidents to the maintenance of the slavery system."

Ironing out the rough wrinkles of what is influencing how we feel about each other is what civilized societies do. White Americans, who do not face what has really happened to our country, are causing themselves to be targeted as a social problem. No one is fooled by the hiding places some choose to go while figuring out how to dismantle other groups. The world has decided that it is comfortable acknowledging whites as a world minority, so that it can move on. Atonement moved South Africans on forward, when they admitted their violent roles while administering apartheid on non-whites.

No one has yet to admit to the role a contorted religion has played then, or now, on modern day freed American slave children. Consider for a moment, religious training in the United States. The European Jews here send their kids to Hebrew School, where their history and Torah are memorized in Yiddish. Christian children spend an hour or so a week hearing carefully animated stories about the life and teachings of a white Jesus. So, the relatives of Black slaves still trust the master's tools hidden within the religion. The historic connection between groups of people is lost when the connection to ancestors has been broken.

I witnessed Black African Mother Mary with her Black African Son is of primal importance in Germany, the Vatican and Turkey. Sacred there, her likeness, as an ancient Egyptian of Nubia is forbidden in the United States. In Genesis 11:1-3, there is documentation that people migrated from Egypt, made agreements for peace between themselves and built other kingdoms elsewhere. The custom that Egypt was a hub from which residents came and went, visited and departed very freely, especially during hard times is documented in Genesis 12. Name changes by conquering armies mislead readers into believing that the Egyptian Empire stopped short of the Fertile Crescent. In fact, it spread out as far east as China, with whom they traded on the Silk Road as far west as the ancient Mali-Ghana-Songhay commonwealth. Genesis clearly documents the movement of various groups in that area for various reasons, which is cross referenced by historical linguists, archaeologists and modern geneticists. In order to pass these events and wisdom along, artisans chiseled mathematical formulae, atomic structures, star clusters, philosophy and more onto the faces of the Egyptian pyramids, while African griots memorized chronologies of bloodlines, as well as historic and geologic events.

Bible references are not all documenting current events of the times. All of Exodus takes place in the East African Empire. In Matthew 1, the reader is reminded of the Old Testament prophecy that reminds us that the leader, Emmanuel will appear as the new leader of Moses's Hebrews. Here is where another of these customary connections is made in the Bible between groups, and their travels back to central Egypt, or somewhere within the Empire. The connection between Mother Mary and her motherland is made when she leaves the territory of King Herod and goes back to Egypt. When King Herod seeks to kill Jesus by killing all other babies, she seeks asylum among her own people. An ancient genocide was put in place against all new male babies to ensure the king's power.

The connection between the Black Africans of Egypt and the Israeli Hebrews is made when Moses leads the Israelis away from Ramses and returns the Hebrews to the Fertile Crescent. Some references are of the ancient societies before what is current Bible conversation, thousands of years before Moses, and two thousand years before Jesus. Moses and his ancestors had a history before he became the receptor of the Ten Commandments. Hebrews and Egyptians were distinguished in Exodus 1. When Moses was found floating in the water by the princess who claimed him as her son, he was trained in the Ancient Egyptian Mystery System. The freed Egyptian slaves were taught by Moses in the wilderness, after they left oppression by Black Egyptians. Exodus 3 has these freed people being delivered into freedom with the Hittites' "spacious land, flowing with milk and honey."

Maintaining racial ghettos has proven valuable as the isolation necessary to rectify social cuing. In forming social cues for oppressive white societies, the ground rules for minority behavior are established. This is not a white practice, but a human practice that should not isolate white humans as defective. Social transactions, left behind when groups change focus can self-propel, becoming self-perpetuated. Scapegoating is a social practice that is not helpful for groups aspiring to rise socially.

In his book, *Revelation and Social Reality,* Paul Lample writes that "Human beings live in social reality as naturally as animals live in the physical world. It is, essentially, invisible. Social reality is an expression of human agreement." So malleable, in itself, that it is in a matter of hours that the whole world is capable of changing from conflict to peace. Individuals are responsible for analyzing social cues to which they daily respond by reflex, without thinking.

*If you are taking this course, now is a good time to read and review the Paul Lample packet.

Symbols Within Ourselves

The Bible uses symbols to impart to the reader the magnitude of Jesus's mission on earth. I have heard such a dramatic reaction from white Christians, making sure that images are used that support their superiority. If Jesus is a symbol lacking melanin, then their own claims to superiority over other humans will be effective. The dispute raises the ire of any white Christian.

Symbols encapsulate the mores of human groups. Because we respond reflexively, it is an effective means to control people. When symbols are rejected, people create new ones. Daring to dispute the symbols of a society dismantles the society at worst. At best, societies redefine themselves. In Daniel 10:6, Jesus is described, "...his arms and legs like burnished bronze...". Revelation 1:14: "The hair on his head was white like wool... His feet were like bronze glowing in a furnace." The description fits the sculptures of the Hittites and others depicted with coiled or locked hair. The term "locks" still refers to hair. A challenge in this American society would be to recall the characteristics of bronze, and admit that it does look like the skin of someone melanin drenched. To put it simply, a very dark brown person. Proceeding further, acquire a bit of bronze, hold a flame to it and see that it glows in its blackness. Top that with some lamb's wool hair and you've got anybody's black-skinned African!

In the gradual effect of the Egyptian Empire being coopted as Greek, the descriptions and depictions of Jesus were required to be whitewashed, if the public were to accept white rule. Eventual separation of Christianity into the Catholic sect did not disavow Mother Mary and her Son as blue-black people with coiled hair. Their representative paintings remain displayed by the Pope as late as 2016.

The bottom line rules of Black inferiority in society have never changed since the formulae were imparted by Willie Lynch's "kit". From the 1700s to presently, the "kit" has not been repealed. Even including the slight alterations offered by ending slavery, ending share cropping and ending Jim Crow laws, the original intent of the "kit" stands. Invisible cues, internalized by the world, regarding the value of some groups over that of others, is the main hand grenade to a lasting peace among human beings. Invisible cues for disenfranchisement do not allow human growth necessary for moving humans into peace. Symbols in American society that cue for white privilege have yet to all be challenged: I was confused when I saw the Confederate Flag flying in 2000. All Christian churches I ever visited use paintings of a white Jesus. The Nazi flag flew on the campus of Merced High School in 2008. A society that instills fear in citizens to control it pits groups against each other, which is moving away from peace. I was quite startled to hear this morning's news, which broadcasted that Arab Muslims, who will be entering the United States as terrorists, will be killing Americans in the streets. The visual was bloody bodies in the streets. That commercial was an invitation to demonize this new group. Black boys in hooded sweat shirts used to be the preferred demons for violence.

African symbols have been adopted as unconscious symbols, such as the staff and serpent to represent American medicine; the Coptic cross to represent Catholics Kinte cloth to represents Scottish plaid, and the energy harnessed by the top of Egyptian pyramids represented by the eye over pyramid on the dollar bill. Subtle symbols affect the unconscious reasoning so that our behavior is predictable to our leadership, but not recognized by the average individual. Contrary to whites, I have experienced Blacks who verbalize distrust and hatred of whites, merely because their skin is white. Those feelings do not cease just because I add that white skin in itself is bad. Whites are bad because they choose vile behaviors. They have the ability to make better choices, but are acting to their own advantage in a society that encourages it.

I always have to refer to the whites in my family, who took their lives into their own hands when conducting on the Underground Railroad. Online research in 2014 cited my white, great-great-grandfather Teakle as a rumor, because they could not corroborate the story with anyone else white, which was humorous to me. Of course no one white knew the set up to free slaves at his house, or none of us would be here to know about it. My grandmother told me never to tell anyone who he was, or anything about him, because we might need a network for freedom again. She also knew racial identity was never to be discussed and never allowed it. When my white or close to white relatives would pass into other groups, I never minded, because they would usually be able to tell me things that could help me. Actually, my most help came from them.

I also have to take up for my Dad's great-grandfather, Governor William Joel Stone, who inherited the land that his family received as soldiers in the Revolutionary War. Everyone else was turning the large plots into plantations for slavery after the war. Well, what did we expect him to do? Also online, I read the story about how the Stones came to the east coast at the request of the Queen of England. My ancestor was run out of town under a city death threat, because he wanted a democracy and the relationship to the Crown. He educated his sons, who are on congressional record as supporting the cause against child labor, oppression of women and Native Americans. He removed some for Europe during the Civil War, which gave his Black son the chance to supply horses to the Union Army. We still have one of the saddles he made from back then.

One route we select to self-reflect is to watch movies. Black American movie makers have justified this effort because they know the harmful effects of symbols and heroes. In the 1970s, sexual symbols were corrected to include Jim Brown, Billy D. Williams, Richard Roundtree, Vonetta McGee, Pamela Grier to name a few. The tragic heroine, Billie Holiday, brought a humanness to movie entertainment, by documenting for the viewer her array of traumatic experiences. It showed illegal drugs introduced to her by her overly demanding employers, police brutalization, lack of public eating, bathroom and sleeping accommodations, and witnessing dead bodies of Black boys and men, hanged from trees by vigilante whites. We now understand that post traumatic shock is a real disorder in need of medical treatment.

However harsh, the movie "Django" shows the analyses and challenges to social cues during African enslavement in the

American south. A black and a white man are seen plotting to circumvent the goals of the invisible cues to reinstate freedom to one enslaved, Brunhilda. The brilliance of the creator of the movie is in depicting the success of recuing key people that were encountered, from the Black butler to the plantation owner.

In the movie "Life", the success of James Dean was because he saw himself as a human being first. Social cues were incidental and could be accepted or not. If faulty, he and his uncle discussed how mixed up a man could become in executing his own life. The fabric of the man would become weak if his own values were unclear, dictated by fantasy and fake living such as in Hollywood.

Years after his plane crash, portraying James Dean as a shiftless daredevil protects our country from having to think. A nervous society had to mislabel him; a misfit because of his rebelliousness. Especially his interest and association with the Black actress, Eartha Kitt, his persona had to be contorted for public consumption. Quite the contrary. When his family values were dropped onto a panorama background of inconsistencies outside the farming town where Dean grew up, the movie made it clear that his reputation must be smeared in order to weaken his image.

Dean's child rearing rendered him able to hold onto life principles that made survival sense. He longed for home, as indicated by his homage to Indiana's poet laureate, James Whitcomb's poem, "We Must Get Home". He shared it in the movie, which kept him centered in his truth and brought him internal peace.

Oscar C. Christensen writes in *Adlerian Family Counseling: A Manual for Counselor, Educator and Psychotherapist,*

"...nearly all child-rearing practices termed 'traditional' and employed on this continent are, in fact, European."

Wondering how that looks from a different continent, it would be apparent that "...the melting pot of America 'melted out' our Asian and African traditions, and have reduced our Indian heritage to a vague memory. The result is that the dominant culture pattern for child-rearing still held as 'American' is, in most respects, European."

Hand in hand with Willie Lynch: "This social order necessitated child training that would ensure children would survive the social system they were growing up to inherit." Psychological symbols of fairness, status, autonomy, certainty and relatedness will have different symbols and elicit different sets of reflexes between various American groups.

In short, some groups may miss out on the essential human need for belonging. A society that isolates groups also loses out on citizens that are loyal or completely bonded to its goals. Nations want sovereignty; the reputation for being able to independently exist. It may take product control, entry restrictions or even war to ensure independence. Groups of citizens that have no belonging feelings will also perhaps not agree with treatment of foreigners. Like the boxer Muhammad Ali declared, why should he go to war and kill people that never called him nigger? Countries run the risk of treason when there is a breach of belongingness. ISIS, the Middle Eastern group, may be provoked to fight because of the documented disenfranchisement of dark nations and groups in Europe and the United States.

Particularly obvious are economic sanctions against Native Americans and African Americans in the US; it used to be said by white southerners, that these sanctions are not unfair. The problem in employment is, Negroes are not hired on jobs due to their lack of education. Blacks fought so hard for this right, that many of its leaders were attacked and some murdered. As late as 2015, the journal "Social Forces" published a study that shows, "Racism is so pervasive in the US job market, that even black Americans with Harvard degrees are at a disadvantage."

University of Michigan sociologist S. Michael Gaddis, asserts that his study even shocked himself, when he discovered Black graduates from Ivy League colleges were recruited at about $4,000 less than white graduates. Also, Black graduates earned no difference in pay without regard for their Ivy League status. In keeping with this American social structure of Willie Lynch's role switch of slave boys and girls, a similar study showed that "black men who signaled on their resumes that they were affiliated with an LGBT group (for example), might overcome anti-black job market bias."

A society that has not relinquished a cued social behavior where men cannot be naturally free or supply their homes has not "recognized their own unconscious biases—nor tried to overcome them." Success for African Americans in the United States is only accomplished when the common structures are circumvented. This is pretty much accepted by and large, inarguably by Blacks, and arguably by whites.

For example, Dr. Mark Dean, Ph.D. is not in the National Hall of Inventors, but, is the architect of the modern day personal computer. Nearly all material products ever created have been from the Black gene set. The Greek persuasion of the world to steal what you want, claim it and praise your own group, is not bringing peace among groups. So many gadgets that we use today were found in archaeological digs in the area Kmt existed. Technology can be lost again if we do not denounce what's in the "kit" for controlling human behavior. Just as we could never fathom attacks on whites around the world by ISIS, we cannot conceive of being hoisted out of power in America either.

Dr Carruthers led the Navy Team that created the space vehicle camera. His patent for the instrument for shortwave energy transmission was in 1969. The camera that went to space was invented in 1972. I had never heard of him until he visited the MAAT Museum of Science in Oakland, California. The article below shows that it wasn't until 2013, under our Black president, that he was given the highest national award in technology.

NRL's Dr. George Carruthers Honored with National Medal of Technology

If you are taking this class, watch Dr. Thomas Mensah in "Fiber Optics" video by Hidden Figures trailer: Nasa's overlooked black female mathematicians

the United States of Africa. He likewise has been omitted from current world celebration.

In fact, after finding out about the Black women in the following video, I felt not as bad that I am usually the only Black science teacher in schools where I have taught outside Detroit. And I also was one of the only "highly qualified" teachers, as well.

Hidden Figures trailer: Nasa's overlooked black female mathematicians

A child's magazine called "Brilliant Star" contributes an interesting approach to changing invisible cuing responses that lead to misunderstanding, violence and destruction. The project is called the "Path to Friendship". The first goal in the journey is to form bonds of true friendship by engaging in meaningful conversation. Next, write down acts of kindness on strips of paper to add to an empty container. Then, pair up with a targeted person for a new friendship. Since the United States government is very aware of groups, use the protected classes from which to pick a friend. Write down 5-10 questions you ever wanted to ask a person in that group. Ask for an interview, so that these questions can be answered. If you have made a friend, he or she will also agree to write down 5-10 questions about you so that you can answer.

Keep conversation going by inviting your friend to an activity with you each week. Don't forget your container of acts of kindness. You can let your friend pick one for you to do at each meeting. Truthful communication is a good way to overcome the inferior-superior model our country is based upon.

To learn more about obstacles in making friends and having meaningful dialogue watch the following YouTube videos:

1. Historic Pedigree of Racism, by Tim Wise

2. History of Class and Race Politics, by Tim Wise

*If you are enrolled in the class for which this book was written, you need to catalogue or record responses from yourself and your new friend on the form from the teacher.